To
Samira Abdel Sayed

EGYPT

Nina Nelson

EGYPT

B. T. Batsford Ltd, London

First published 1976
© Nina Nelson 1976

ISBN 0 7134 3181 4
Computer typeset by
Input Typesetting Ltd, London SE1
Printed in Great Britain by
Biddles Ltd, Guildford, Surrey
for the publishers
B. T. Batsford Ltd, 4 Fitzhardinge Street, London W1H 0AH

Contents

The illustrations

Acknowledgments

I wish to express my deep gratitude to His Excellency Ibrahim Naguib, the Egyptian Tourist Minister, who made me so welcome in his country. I am beholden also to Adel Taher, Under-Secretary of State for Tourism, for his interest and help during the gathering of information for this book. His discussion with me on Akhenaton's monotheism, centuries before our own beliefs were crystallized, was fascinating.

My thanks are due to other members of the Egyptian Tourist Administration, amongst them: Samir el Boereky; Nabil Hanzal; Aboul Wafa; Salwa Fakhny; Lamie Abdo; Farouk Khalid; Roda el Zayadi; Hassan Hashem, Director General of the Publicity Department; Nadia Ibrahim, Director of the Alexandria Office; and Galal Eid, Director of the Luxor Office. In particular I wish to thank Aly Kahala, the Tourist Director in Aswan, who not only arranged my visit this time but introduced me to Aswan first some ten years ago. My thanks to Ali Gohar of Egyptian television and Tawfik Souidan who led me astray on visits to the better-known night spots.

I am indebted to Samir Raouf, former Tourist Attaché in London; to Youssef Hanna Shehata, Director of the Alexandria Museum, and Abdel Haleem Mohammed the Egyptologist who showed me around sites near Minia. Also Abdel Rahman el Sayed, Director of Public Relations in Assiut.

My thanks to Sayed el Nahas for an unforgettable visit to the Egyptian vineyards, to Mohammed el Mahdi who showed me around Assiut and Minia, and Kamal Naguib of *Al*

Ahram. Among the helpful hoteliers I met were Antoine Castani, Sayed Hosni, Naguib Iskander, Marwan Labib and Mr Raina. Emil Tawfik and Ted Woodhams of Egypt Air's London office produced flights of fancy and brought me down to earth as required!

My knowledge of and enthusiasm for Egyptology were enhanced by meetings with Dr Mouktar and Dr Henry Riad. I am most grateful to Ahmed Zakki of EGOTH who was not only his usual zealous self about future hotel plans but was never nonplussed by my many requests; also Abdel Khalek Anwar of the same organization. My grateful thanks as well to Rashad Ghazal, chairman of the Upper Egypt Hotels Company.

In London, where the idea of this book was planned, I am greatly obliged to Sami el Masri, the Tourist Attaché of the Egyptian Embassy. He smoothed my path in every direction and was kind enough to read the manuscript of this book.

My thanks as always to Marie Chitty who deciphers my manuscript and miraculously turns it into a book!

For permission to use photographs I would like to thank: Gerry Brenes and Feature-pix for Pl. 24; Douglas Dickens for Pls 3, 7, 10-12, 17; the Egyptian State Tourist Administration Pl. 8; A. F. Kersting for Pls. 1, 2, 4-6, 13-15, 20-23. Plates 9, 16, 18 and 19 are from my own collection.

EGYPT

MEDITERRANEAN SEA

Sidi Barrani
Ras el
Hekma
Sollum
Mersa Matruh
Sidi Abdel
Rahman
Alamein
Rosetta
Alexandria
Tanta
L. Manzala
Damietta
Port Said
Gaza
Rafah
El Qantara
Wadi el Natrun
L. Timsah
Banha
Ismailia
*Bitter
Lakes*
El Quseima
Qattara
Qattara Depression
SIWA OASIS
Siwa
Delta Barrage
El Giza
Sakkara
CAIRO
Helwan
Ain
Sokhna
Suez
S I N A I
L. Qarun
El Fayoum
Beni Suef
Abu Zneima
Abu Rudeis
Gebel Musa
Nile
EASTERN
Ras Gharib
Gulf of Suez
WESTERN
El Minya
Beni Hassan
Mallawi
Tel el Amarna
Ain Dalla
Assiut
Assiut Barrage
Hurghada
*RED
SEA*
Qasr el Farafra
DESERT
FARAFRA OASES
D E S E R T
Suhag
Abydos
El Baliana
Nag Hammadi
Hatshepsut
Ramesseum
Medinet Habu
Denderah
Qena
*Colossi of
Memnon*
Luxor
El Karnak
DAKHLA OASES
Esnah
Esnah
Edfu
Horus
KHARGA OASES
Kom Ombo
Aswan
Aswan Dam
Kalabsha
Philae
Dakka
Lake
Nasser
Abu Simbel

0 20   100   200 miles
   50 100   300 km
▲ temples

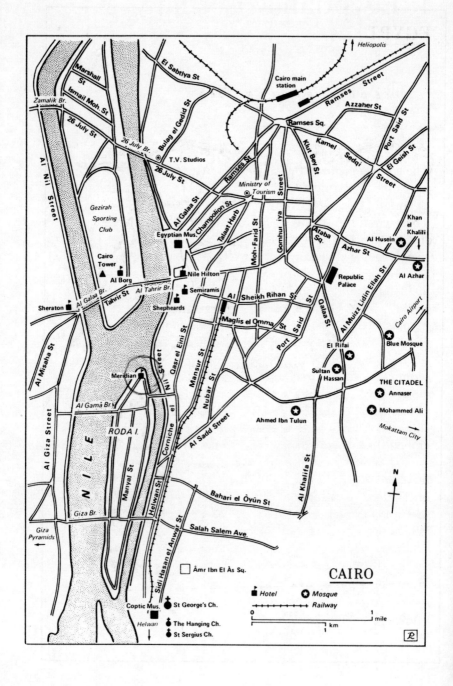

CAIRO

Hotel •   Mosque ✪

0   Railway +++++++++ 1 mile

1 km

1 Egyptian Miscellany

The earliest civilized people on this planet, as far as we know, were the Egyptians. Back in the days of Abraham the Egyptians had settled laws and an established government. Their country was as beautiful and unique as today – a shallow, narrow valley of incredible fertility divided by the river Nile and edged by burning desert and bare hills.

The sun shines continually on the land. The Nile is its lifeblood. From the cool depths of the river sprang many of the world's first religions. Aeons ago it was believed that in paradise Isis wept for her lost Osiris and her tears caused water to flow earthward into the Nile because, miraculously, the river rose each year. Water overflowed the banks, left rich sediment for the crops and then subsided. Cities flourished along the magic river, aglitter with temples, statues, monuments, stelae of lapis lazuli and obelisks whose summits shone with inlay work of gold and silver. Succeeding princes embellished them further and word of their magnificence spread. It was natural that when man developed the desire to travel he should be drawn to Egypt. There was the Kingdom of Thebes, of Elephantine, of Abydos and the Kingdom of Memphis, which embraced the western half of the delta. When the great Theban kings came to the fore the others gradually assumed the rank of sovereign priests.

The history of Greece begins with the Trojan War. However, centuries before that the power of Thebes had passed away – but not its glory. The columns which still uphold the temples were later copied by the Greeks. Egyptian gods were adopted by the Romans. The great monuments and tombs and the fantastic pyramids of the delta have, for the last 3000 years, made Egypt a place of fascination for the traveller.

Without doubt the thing that will strike the present-day tourist first is the way the new blends with the old. Up-to-date Cairo for instance, with its skyscrapers, television centre, modern university, espresso bars and boutiques, rubs shoulders with ancient mosques. Al Azhar – the oldest university in the world – and the trading alleys of the Mousky, where skilled craftsmen work as their fathers did before them. It is the same throughout the country. The old is sharply divided from the new as the delta from the desert.

The tourist often feels he has skimmed the cream off Egypt if he visits Cairo, Luxor and Aswan, but there are other fascinating places and all with the same dry sunny climate: the oasis of the Fayoum, a sportsman's paradise less than a morning's drive from Cairo; the sunny beaches like Mersa Matruh, with pale golden sand; the coast of the Red Sea where skin diving and deep-sea fishing are second to none. There is Assiut, Siwa, Alexandria with its catacombs and Tanagra figurines – and many more besides.

Individual visitors want different things. Those interested in ancient monuments may wonder which of the many temples along the Nile to visit, those who loathe museums want to know the best and most exotic nightspots. Ballet lovers may like to see folk dancing, engineers to visit the Aswan Dam and sun worshippers wish to know the best beach for a sun tan. For these as well as other travellers Egypt has much to offer. A modern network of communications is at the disposal of tourists, which includes aircraft, air-conditioned trains, hydrofoil boats and floating hotels.

Unfortunately there is not enough space to mention all the places and monuments that would interest visitors. I cannot explain this more aptly than by quoting a remark made by Lawrence of Arabia. 'You can see more in Egypt in one year, than anywhere else in ten.'

Egyptian history is long and involved – but fascinating. In a thumbnail sketch it is difficult to know where to begin, and much must be left out. As half the joy in visiting the ancient monuments is to know something of their background, it is as well to have an idea of the various dynasties, gods and goddesses.

Some 30 centuries elapsed from the building of the Pyramids to the Roman Conquest. The Egyptians recorded their history during this time in dynasties – each dynasty being a line of hereditary rulers. The Tablet of Abydos (discovered during Mariette's excavations in 1864 in the temple of Osiris at Abydos and equal in importance to the Rosetta Stone) gives a list of 75 of these Pharaohs, beginning with Mena, 4400 B.C., and ending with Seti I, 1300 B.C. The latter is believed by many to have been the Pharaoh of the Exodus.

For the sake of convenience historians have divided the dynasties into three periods.

The Ancient Empire   (11 dynasties)
The Middle Kingdom   (9 dynasties)
The New Kingdom   (10 dynasties)

Then came the rule of the Persians, Macedonians, Ptolemies and Romans followed by the Arab conquest in A.D. 641.

In dynastic times those talented in any of the arts flourished as they never have before or since. They were held in veneration second only to Pharaoh himself. Pharaohs held among their splendid titles that of 'Scribe of the Sun' and nobles who could neither read nor write used the words 'Scribe' as a distinguished appellation. Architects and artists were allowed unlimited gold to build and decorate monuments.

Senmut, royal architect during the reign of Queen Hatshepsut, became one of the queen's chief advisers because of the magnificent temples he designed.

Pharaoh Amenophis had an extremely gifted architect of the same name, who was actually considered a god and whose sayings were still being quoted 1200 years after his death.

Architecturally the Pharaonic temples followed a similar

pattern. They were approached by long avenues lined with stone figures. The entrance, called a pylon, was an H-shaped construction, its sides slanting slightly inward. Spreading wings of the god Horus were carved above the lintel of the high doorways. The pylon led to an open court edged on three sides by a colonnade. A vast pillared hall beyond was called the hypostyle hall; this in turn led to chambers and passages. In the heart of the temple was the shrine where a figure of the god was jealously guarded. Inside the temple precincts was a sacred lake in which the royal barge was placed on special occasions and where the priests purified themselves before ceremonies. Except for statues, the only forms of decoration in the temples were carvings on the walls and columns. These portray Pharaohs making suitable offerings to the gods, who give back in return strength, life and happiness. The figures are rigid, dignified and formal and are in sharp contrast to the lively reliefs showing scenes from royal daily life.

The visitor will notice that the carvings are always in profile. In the few exceptions to this the work is not of the same quality or even in proportion – for instance in the female form the breast is under the arm. In statues the left profile is more delicate than the right. The sculptor only traced the left side of the face on the block and left the rest to be carved by his apprentices.

Pharaonic gods are many and difficult to catalogue. Some are replicas of each other and many have the same characteristics.

Ra was the self-begotten great Sun-God, also called Amen Ra. His son was Osiris. Osiris ruled wisely on earth but was murdered by Set, his brother, God of Darkness. Osiris was resurrected. Osiris and Isis begat Horus. Horus became Lord of the Earth and Osiris God of the Underworld, Judge of the Dead.

During religious ceremonies priests would put on animal masks when representing gods, for each god not only possessed all virtues of the human but also a particular attribute from an animal or bird. Sekmet, the God of War, had the strength of the lion, Anubis the fleetness of the jackal, and Horus the keen sight of the hawk. The hawk's association with the Sun-God is always used and easily understood, for the hawk could soar into the sky and his eye did not flinch from the sun.

The short list that follows gives the name of the favourite symbol associated with the best-known individual deities:

Amen Ra	the hawk and the ram
Anubis	the jackal
Bast	the cat
Hathor	the cow
Horus	the hawk
Khnum	the ram
Mut	the vulture
Ptah	the bull
Thoth	the ibis

Hieratic and demotic characters require much study but the tourist will be able to understand the pictorial writing on temple walls with a little practice. For instance gods and goddesses can be recognised by their head dresses. Emblems of rule, sovereignty and dominion are represented by the crook, sceptre and the flail.

EMBLEMS

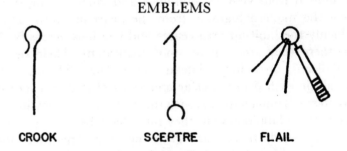

| CROOK | SCEPTRE | FLAIL |

The symbol of the Key of Life is shown thus:

After the amalgamation of Upper and Lower Egypt the double crown is worn:

First on the tourist's list when in Cairo is a visit to the Pyramids and that most famous of all stone figures – the Sphinx. It is difficult to describe the immensity of the Pyramids. Writers have been trying to do this since Herodotus. To quote their actual measurements does not help, although to describe what could be contained in them, or what could be made if they were dismantled, gives some indication.

The example I like best is by Napoleon's mathematician, Monge, who worked out that masonry in the three important Pyramids at Giza would be sufficient to enclose the whole area of France with a wall, one foot thick and ten feet high!

The first glance at the Pyramids is an unexpected one. They are hidden from view by buildings and villas as you drive along the modern highway from the heart of Cairo. Then suddenly the built-up area ceases and you look across fields and there they are – great stone mountains. Their site is magnificent, on a high plateau above Cairo. Through the crystal air each detail is clear and you feel that you merely have to reach out a hand to touch them. It is almost possible to visualize the fabulous sight they must have been before they were damaged, their sides glittering with limestone and decorated with reliefs while at their feet lay the Sphinx, priceless ornaments hanging from her head, her face painted a brilliant red. The casing has long since gone but some still caps the second pyramid, and at its gigantic base I have picked up several small pieces.

I said it was difficult to describe the immensity of the Pyramids, but as you walk along their bases and put your

1. *Cairo minarets with the minaret of the Aqsunqur mosque in the foreground*

head back to glance up along their colossal sides, you can sense it and you feel the size of an ant.

One hundred thousand men, says Herodotus, toiled for 20 years, quarrying the Mokattam Hills, dragging blocks of stone across desert and Nile and finally piled them – accurately shaped and dressed – layer upon layer until the Great Pyramid of Cheops was made. A whole nation did this at the bidding of one man whom they thought to be a god.

The inside is no less fantastic. The entrance is on the north side, some 50 feet above ground level. You climb bent double up a steep passage 128 feet long and, in spite of electric light and a handrail, you feel more than a little apprehensive. Continuing along a corridor just over three feet high you reach the Pharaoh's burial chamber of black granite. This contains the King's red granite sarcophagus. Above there are four horizontal stone ceilings separated by empty spaces and topped by further triangular roofing, thus protecting the chamber, the guide says, from pressure above us! There is also a Queen's chamber. I do not recommend elderly people to go into the Great Pyramid and certainly not to climb the outside. Indeed the latter is dangerous for anyone and is frowned upon, although people continue to do it despite serious accidents.

The other two large pyramids of the Giza group were built for Chephren (2650 B.C.) and Mycerinus (2600 B.C.) The latter cannot be climbed or entered by visitors.

Chephren, Cheops' son, built his pyramid next to his father's to the south-west. It is somewhat smaller and as has been mentioned, still retains some original casing. Two temples belonging to it have been excavated and can be visited. The pyramid appears to many to be larger than that of Cheops because it stands on a higher level of stone foundation. It has two openings in the north side, one a corridor of 105 feet which leads into the funerary chamber, and the other, 100 feet long, first descends and then ascends and also leads to the funerary chamber where you can see Chephren's sarcophagus. An ascent of this pyramid is far more difficult than that of Cheops.

2. Sharia Sukkariya with Zuweila Gate and the twin minarets of Mosque El M'Ayyad in the background

The sarcophagus from Mycerinus' pyramid was lost in a wreck on its way to England, but several fragments were saved and are in the British Museum.

The Sphinx is close to the Chephren pyramid, her expression patient, wholly mysterious. 3,733 years before Christ, during the reign of Cheops, her body lay hidden, blanketed by desert sand, but her head gazed out over the Nile with its famed inscrutability.

The Sphinx does not try to impress you; quietly she lies there hiding her past, unmindful of the future. Her fame is proclaimed in poem and book, sometimes extravagantly, at other times with simplicity, sometimes even with amusement. Compton Mackenzie likened her to a kitten in a bath! In the weekly tourist leaflet, *This Week in Cairo,* she is dismissed in the brief phrase, 'The Sphinx lies beside the Pyramids'. She has been painted by artists of every nationality and there are men who make a living out of shading your camera lens by hand while you take her photograph. Like any international beauty her age is uncertain. Although there are stories about her there are few facts. It is said that her nose was damaged by artillery during the Napoleonic campaign, but even this does not detract from the dignity of her face. Between her paws lies a stele which relates the following tale in hieroglyphics. While in a deep sleep King Thothmes IV saw the God Harmachis. The God promised to bestow the crown of Egypt on his head should he excavate the stone statue from the encroaching desert. It was in 1466 that this King released the Sphinx's body from beneath a deep covering of sand. Because of this stele many Egyptologists believe that the Sphinx represents Harmachis, the God of the Morning. In 1905 the haunches and the great paws of the Sphinx were excavated.

Her lion's body stretches some 150 feet, her paws are 50 feet long, the head is 30 feet long, the face is 14 feet wide – yet she is small, truly minute in comparison to the vast hulks of the Pyramids. Her lion's tail is curled up, like a cat's, over one great haunch.

Without question the most rewarding place to go after dark is to see the Son et Lumière presentation of the Sphinx and the

Pyramids. You can watch from an open air threatre while 5,000 years of splendour live again. Coloured searchlights soften the vast outlines of the monuments against a warm sky spattered with stars, crickets chatter constantly and an occasional desert dog barks from far away in the sands. The lights fade and brighten, music and stereophonic voices turn the pages of history and one particular sentence hangs on the air, 'Man fears Time – but Time fears the Pyramids'. The dialogue is in different languages on successive evenings.

From Cairo the drive out to the Pyramids along the same road originally made by the Khedive Ismail for the Empress Eugenie when she wished to visit the famous monuments, takes about twenty minutes. You can go by taxi or a number 8 bus from the south side of Liberation Square. If the latter you get out at a stop near the Pyramids where a special bus provides a shuttle service to the open-air theatre.

Of the many outstanding Pharaohs none is more fascinating than Amenophis IV (1370-1352 B.C.) He later changed his name to Akhnaton when he renounced the gods and goddesses of Thebes and replaced them with one god, the Sun Disk, the 'Aton', symbolic of spiritual goodness, happiness and love. The priests were astounded and continued in their own beliefs while Akhnaton founded his new city of Tell el Armana on the east bank of the Nile. Eighty thousands citizens joined him. His wife, the beautiful Nefertiti, also upheld his Aton belief. This monotheistic cult was 1,000 years in advance of our own religions and many of the Aton's hymns of praise are similar to those in the Koran or the Bible. Thus

Thou appearest resplendent on the horizons of the heavens, thou living sun who wast the first to live. Thou arisest on the eastern horizon and fillest the earth with thy beauty . . . All the flocks are content in their pastures. The trees and herbs become green, the birds flutter in their nests and lift their wings to praise thee. All creatures leap upon their feet; all that flutter and fly, live when thou arisest for them.

In the new city of the sun a great temple was built to Aten.

Few traces of it remain today, although it is known that it was 2409 feet long and 90½ feet wide. Indeed little remains of this city except delightful scenes of family life of the Pharaoh, Nefertiti and their little daughters which are on tomb walls. The royal couple are seen sacrificing to the sun whose rays often terminate in tiny hands stretched out to bless the royal couple and the princesses.

There is a granite head of Nefertiti in the Cairo museum but not as beautiful as the famous 'Green Head' which is in the Berlin Museum. Who has not seen at least pictures of this bust of Nefertiti whose loveliness exceeded even that of Cleopatra. The head was excavated with other finds in 1912 by a German Egyptologist, Dr Ludwig Boregart.

During the Second World War it was carefully encased in glass wool and hidden with other treasures in the salt mines of the Harz mountains. An American G.I. discovered it in 1945 and for the second time in history the lovely head emerged from the very bowels of the earth.

Beneath a sweeping eyebrow the onlooker can see that the queen has a cataract in one eye yet, despite this disfigurement, unusual in one so young, the head remains the epitome of beauty.

One of Nefertiti's daughters was to marry Tutankhamen and when the latter became Pharaoh he returned to Thebes and to the old religions and Tell el Amarna was forgotten.

Persian rule lasted from 525 to 404 B.C. in Egypt. Cambyses was crowned King and took all the titles of the Pharaoh, Darius I was to follow. The Persians respected the religion of the Egyptians which gained them much support. The Greek period came next. Napoleon later said 'By the foundation of Alexandria, Alexander has increased his fame more than by his victories. It was the city which was to become the heart of the universe.'

Then came the Roman Emperors, and traditions continued to be respected. It was during Byzantine rule that destruction swept through the ancient cities of Egypt. It was a time when buildings, monuments and temples were destroyed. Some were converted into churches or monasteries. Then in A.D. 638

the Arabs led by Amr conquered Egypt and introduced the Islamic religion.

The capital of Egypt did not bear the name of Cairo until the time of the Fatimid Caliphs (the Fatimids considered themselves direct descendants of Fatima, daughter of the Prophet Mohammed). They wrested the country from the Abbasids in A.D. 969 and foundations were laid for a walled city to house the Caliph. It was called Al-Qahira (the Triumphant) and eventually became Cairo. The city has inherited several architectural monuments from the Fatimid Caliphs, notably the Mosque of Al-Azhar. It forms part of the oldest university in the world. The Rector and his staff wear the same type of robe that tutors have worn for a thousand years, dark blue galabias, a long loose robe of fine wool and white turbans. Teaching is based on the Koran and Moslem students gather there from all over the Near and Far East in their thousands.

In A.D. 980 the vizier, Yacub Ibn Killis, author of a highly regarded religious manuscript, would read aloud in Al Azhar mosque. Because of this it became politic for others to do likewise. Finally several jurists were appointed to conduct additional studies there, and so the university began.

The original rectangular form of the building is still the same, though, after an earthquake in 1303, the mosque had to be rebuilt. Frequent restorations and additions have been made down through the centuries but the character of the building has been preserved. Charity has always been part of Al Azhar's tradition, the blind were cared for and even up to a century ago it was estimated that no less than 40,000 individuals would call every alternate day, when 3,800 pounds of bread and a quantity of oil for lamps would be distributed.

The university is a vast place, irregular in shape, with long avenues of columns. Students in hundreds of groups have their places reserved under niches and porticoes where they gather around their tutors.

Beautiful hand-woven red carpets, with scrolled medallions in the centres, are strewn over the stone floors. Students remove their shoes but tourists are invited to wear felt overshoes before they walk into the vaulted halls. The oldest praying niche is in a beautifully proportioned rectangular hall whose ceiling is supported by 140 pillars. The library is a remarkable one, possessing 52,000 volumes, of which some 15,000 are manuscripts, many of them priceless. A certificate of Specialization takes some three years to obtain, one of Proficiency eight years and a Doctorate twelve years.

The Door of the Barbers (there are eight entrances) in the western facade leads towards the main courtyard and from here you can see the detail of the three beautiful minarets. Many visitors ask where the concept of the minaret came from. When the Moslems first came to Egypt the Pharos lighthouse in Alexandria, one of the seven wonders of the ancient world, was still standing. One of the chambers at the top was transformed into a place of worship. This was an unusual concept but so in keeping with the thought of prayer ascending that from it grew the idea of the minaret (the Arabic for lighthouse is *minar*) which all mosques had in future. In turn it was from the Moslem minaret that Christian churches developed the steeple.

A minaret is usually square from its base to the top of the mosque's wall, then octagonal above. The upper portion is divided into two or three parts, the top storey being set back to make room for the balcony from which the call to prayer is chanted. To give greater width to the balcony it is corbelled out with stalactitic vaulting. The top has a small dome. In the case of the three minarets of Al Azhar, each is different in design, the most lovely having as its zenith a double dome.

Having heard of the cramped quarters of Al Azhar, one is astonished at the spaciousness of the university. As tourists cannot visit during teaching hours or the hours of prayer, this is understandable as the students have dispersed when it is open to the public. Nevertheless quarters are cramped. For instance, during lecture hours, one small roofed-over chamber has four corners with students from different countries in each. Because there are so many young people and so little space, the university has spread and student hostels are dotted about Cairo. An illusion of space is created by many of the larger courtyards being open to the sky.

You cannot truly appreciate the Middle East unless you know a little about Islam. It is a religion more like Christianity than any other. The Koran is the Moslem Bible. Glance through its pages and you will meet old biblical friends like Abraham, Noah and Moses.

Mohammed was born some 500 years after Christ. He studied the life of Jesus and acknowledged the binding force of his teachings as a great prophet. One difference between the two creeds is the way the Mohammedan worships in public, while the Christian, except in church, worships in private. At any time of day, in a crowded street or in the country you may see a Mohammedan go down on his knees, with or without a prayer mat, to make his obeisance to God. This is done so naturally that you feel strangely humbled by the sight. The driver of your car may draw up to the side of the road and ask you if you will excuse him for a few minutes while he says his prayers.

The words 'Allah is great and Mohammed is his Prophet' are sung from countless minarets by priests five times each day, to remind people of God. Each believer is required to work out his own salvation. According to a religious writer, Sayed Ameer Aly, 'Each soul rises to its Creator without the intervention of priest or hierophant. Each human being is his own priest, in the Islam of Mohammed no man is higher than the other.'

Another difference between Christian and Mohammedan is that the former tries to bend fate to his will, the Mohammedan feels everything is preordained. Life has certain things in store for him. He will try and place his footsteps one way but if they diverge, even slightly, he knows it is God's will. God knows best. *'Elhamdo l'Allah'* you hear on all sides of Egypt, 'Thanks be to God'; or *'En sha Allah'*, 'If it is God's will,' The latter is often used instead of saying 'yes'.

Ramadan is to the Mohammedan what Lent is to the Christian but far more stringent. It begins when the new moon rises in the ninth month of the Mohammedan year; from then for 28 days a strict fast from dawn to sunset is observed. The sick and ailing do not fast, neither do small children or old people and there are various conditions when there is dispensation for people who ordinarily fast – for instance when travelling.

A third difference between the two religions is in the attitude towards cemeteries. The Mohammedan burial grounds often look like small villages with rounded domes of white, pale blue or apricot. Many Mohammedans save during their life for such a resting place so that when they are dead their children and friends will visit their tomb on feast days, eat there (food not consumed is left for the poor) and feel that once again they are close together. The Mohammedan is very generous to the needy.

The Copts are the direct descendants of the ancient Egyptians and bear an amazing resemblance to the figures carved on the walls of the Pharaonic tombs, temples and monuments. They number more than a million persons and are Christian – furthermore they were among the earliest Christians. In A.D. 64 Saint Mark ordained one Ananius, Patriarch of Alexandria, and the city became a Christian centre. Two hundred years later Saint Anthony withdrew from Alexandria to the desert to abstain from worldly things. There he taught his Christian followers to lead an ascetic life and so started the first monastery.

The Copts' own language., Coptic, fell to disuse after the Mohammedan invasion in the seventh century, but is still used for liturgical purposes. The Copts are not subject to Rome but make use of confession, which is obligatory before receiving the Eucharist. During services the clergy and choir occupy the part of the church containing the altar, the male congregation sit in a second compartment and the women sit by themselves in a third. A screen separates each.

The head of the Coptic church was for centuries the Patriarch of Alexandria but is now the Patriarch of Cairo. His jurisdiction also extends over the Church in Abyssinia.

The majority of Egypt's population are farmers – the *fellaheen*. The Koran says 'Man cannot exist without constant effort' and this might well be their adage. Aided by highly organized irrigation, the growth of crops is so rapid that the *fellah* is constantly tending his soil. Clad in his long cotton robe and small skull cap, there is no more picturesque site along the Nile and canals than that of the fellah working in the fields. He is lean and of medium height. Beneath straight eyebrows his sunburnt face is thin, with high cheekbones. Physically he still resembles the drawings on temple walls.

Ploughing is done by the traditional yoke of oxen or buffalo. The plough, called a *zahhafa,* its point iron-shod, is merely a long pole of wood, perhaps the trunk of a tree. It does not pierce the soil deeply but probes it sufficiently for seed to take root, and such is the richness of the land that during the space of a year several crops can be grown from the same plot.

The staple food of the fellah is unleavened bread filled with *fool* – a type of haricot bean which is the hardiest of the Egyptian vegetables.

He grows bercime, an emerald green clover, for his animals. First of all the soil is covered by some three inches of water, than the seed is sown broadcast. When the water has been absorbed into the ground the seed germinates on the surface and with no delay sprouts its thin green stalk sunward. Sometimes the animals are brought to the bercime rather than bringing the fodder to the animals.

You will often catch a glimpse of vivid colour in the laundry of the womenfolk when they wash their clothing at the river's edge, for although the men wear white galabias and the women an outer dress of black, beneath they have gaudy colours. Sunset is the favourite time of day for the women. It is when they gossip and talk while they launder or clean their copper cooking pots on the banks of the Nile. This is where they live the social part of their life, for since early morning they have been busy with domestic duties or helping their menfolk in the fields.

In spite of sweeping black attire from head to foot it is with ease that the fellah's wife bends to the river, fills her water pot to the brim and, without spilling a single droop, lifts it into the air and balances it on her head. Then she walks home with a grace and dignity that has been handed down by her forebears. A glamorous touch, denoting the wealth of her family, is sometimes suggested by gold or gilded coins suspended from a veil covering the lower part of her face. She is given an anklet of silver, perhaps of gold, at her wedding. Tourists can seldom buy antique anklets for they are venerated far more highly than wedding rings or bracelets.

The great curse of the fellaheen is bilharzia, a complaint far more violent than malaria or dysentery. It is caused by worms that thrive in the mud of the canals. The bug penetrates the skin and settles in the kidneys where it devitalizes even the strongest of men. Great efforts have been made to stamp it out but it is a slow battle and research is carried on to discover methods of control.

In spite of this handicap the fellah continues to be one of the strongest agricultural workers in the world. It was due to him that the granaries were filled throughout the seven years of famine recorded in the Bible. Later, it was through him that Egypt became the granary of Rome during the days of the Roman Empire. The fellah knows the seasons like the back of his hand and the exact productivity of his soil.

During the hottest part of the year farming activities are often done at night, for when the moon is full it is nearly as bright as day and the air is cool. It is strange that the fellah should stay in or near the village where he was born and have no desire to roam when his brother the Beduin leads a nomad existence. The roving Beduin has a more romantic appeal to the visitor, but it is the fellah who is the mainstay of Egypt.

The camel is the creature that one has associated with Egypt since childhood, and family photograph albums show great uncle George sitting on a camel with a background of the Giza Pyramids; turn the next page and there is father doing the same thing and you will probably do it too!

The camel still plays a part in the economy of the country. He holds his head in such a disdainful manner because it is said that although Man knows ninety-nine names for Allah the camel knows the hundredth! The weight he can carry is phenomenal and his slithering cushion footed gait enables him to plod with equal ease over the burning steeets of the city or with the sand tugging at his heels in the desert. Without him the Beduin could not exist, for the skin provides the Beduin tent and leather, the wool his rugs and burnous and camel dung is used for camp fires. The camel possesses more endurance than any other creature and will not flag until he is at the end of his tether. Nothing will resuscitate him at this stage – hence 'the straw that broke the camel's back'.

Visitors who enjoy riding will find the Arab horse a fine one (there are excellent stables near the Pyramids of Giza). The Arab chiefs have never used their horses as beasts of burden but only for hunting and war. Abbas Pasha the First was said to have a stable of horses more beautiful than any since the days of King Solomon. Great interest has always been taken in breeding. It was not customary for Mohammedans to take stud money and the breed so improved that today the world's best stables boast Arab blood.

Beduin horse dancing is fascinating. The horsemanship is superb and in the old tradition but I have watched an equestrian display where the riders were dressed as cowboys! With lassoos whirling above their heads they give a rowdy display of a steer roundup as exciting on the sands of the desert as it would be on the plains of Texas.

Hardier than the horse, but a very humble cousin, is the donkey. You see this gentle creature everywhere and, with his long amusing ears and tuft of a tail, it seems a pity that he should be an emblem of stupidity and ignorance, for any task he is called upon to do he does obediently. A donkey can still be bought for as little as ten pounds.

Wherever there is arable land there is also the buffalo, who turns the water wheel, pulls the plough, gives milk and is more disease resistant than the cow. He is to the fellah what the camel is to the Beduin.

Fellaheen women shepherd the sheep and lead their flocks, contrary to our custom of driving them. The Middle Eastern sheep are attractive in appearance, except for their very fat cumbersome tails. As the camel stores food and drink in his extra stomach, so these sheep store extra food in their tails. At market tail fat is the cheapest part of the carcass and is sold to be used as cooking fat.

Gazelles, jackals and ibex are found in the Western Desert. Of the reptile family there are lizards, geckos and chameleons. I have seen the sloughed off skins of snakes but have never met one. Scorpions are numerous but again you cannot often see them. However, it is advisable to be cautious near thickets or piles of stones.

Migratory birds are numerous and vary in size from stork to quail. Of birds of prey the kite constantly wheels overhead, the sun piercing his fully spread wings so that he gleams like cornelian velvet. He plunges to the earth quickly and, like the eagle, clutches his prey with his claws. He keeps disease at bay in his endless quest for food. It is not only offal he collects; his taste is often that of an epicure for he has been known to plunge down in elegant gardens while a meal is being served in the open air and fly off again with delicacies from the table.

Egrets are protected. They follow the fellah's plough, their wings pure white against the brown earth. When evening comes they gather together and a whole flock will suddenly fly into one tree and nestle in among the branches for the night. In the half light these bird laden trees appear as though blossoming with huge white flowers.

Lantana, a lover of sandy soil, grows all over the country as does bougainvillea. There are cacti of every kind from the prickly pear, the pods of which are sold and eaten, to tiny exotic ones with flame coloured flowers. The prickly pears, their thick fleshy stems covered with clusters of spikes, line the desert roads side by side with an attractive rose-shaped cactus with fat petals, like those of a Jerusalem artichoke. These grow in clusters close to the ground and pink flowers blossom from the green petals.

In the desert the seeds and their behaviour are as different from those of the cultivated flower as black from white. One is the stork bill, a bright purple blossom with a dark flare at its base. When the petals fall they reveal a spike which grows to form the 'stork bill'. This splits into feathered tails enclosing a seed. They blow away. As a tail dries the part nearest the head twists up. A drop of water can cause this to untwist. At night the slightest drop of dew has this effect and the alternate damping by night and drying by day screws the tiny pointed head into the sand. The desert honesty seed is affected by dew too and becomes sticky immediately, then adheres and burrows into the sand. After a heavy dew the wadis become light green and all sorts of flowers appear. Egyptian sage is one of the most vivid ones. It is a mauve flower encased in blue. The leaves being small and nondescript, huddle close to the sand, while the flower stands boldly upright as if challenging the sky to outshine its periwinkle blue. The Beduin use sage for the cure of gastro-intestinal trouble. Nothing is wasted in the desert — least of all the bitter apple. This grows to the size of an ordinary apple and is dark green at first then changes to a golden creamy colour. The flowers are pretty and trail along the ground in masses pale yellow. The seeds are nourishing and are used as food by the Beduin. He also roasts them and with the liquid smears his goatskin water bottle to make it watertight.

For a country so sparsely wooded Egypt has a variety of trees, acacias, sycamores, tamarisk, eucalyptus, and all kinds of fruit trees. Flamboyants line the avenues and parks, a dazzling sight in the bright sun with their flame coloured flowers and glossy green leaves. I prefer the jacarandas. Their blossoms of powder blue look cool against the deeper blue of the sky and, during the nights of the full moon, they turn an exotic mauve.

The Egyptian climate is predictable and very pleasant throughout the year. The winter (14th November is supposed to begin this season) is the most popular time. This is understandable when you consider that, while we are shovelling snow, wearing raincoats or peering through fog, Egypt is enjoying spring-like weather and getting eight hours' sunshine a day! Spring (March to May) and autumn (September to November) are seasons of stable, warm weather and sunny skies.

In summer (June to August) the heat of the day is modified by the cool northerly winds from Europe across the Mediterranean. The low degree of humidity makes this season most agreeable for those who enjoy hot weather.

Khamsin conditions do not occur often and then only for brief periods. This is when hot gusty winds in the desert stir up great sheets of sand that cloud the sky over. Rain is practically non-existent.

AVERAGE AIR TEMPERATURES IN CENTIGRADE

MINIMUM

MEAN MINIMUM AIR TEMPERATURE °C

Town	Jan.	Feb.	Mar.	April	May	June	July	Aug.	Sept.	Oct.	Nov.	Dec.
Cairo	8.6	9.3	11.3	13.9	17.4	17.9	21.5	21.6	19.9	17.8	13.9	10.4
Alexandria	9.3	9.7	11.2	13.5	16.7	20.2	22.7	22.9	21.3	17.8	14.8	11.2
Mersa Matruh	8.1	8.4	9.7	11.8	14.5	18.2	20.2	21.0	19.7	16.8	13.3	10.0
Port-Said	11.3	12.1	13.5	16.1	19.6	22.4	24.1	24.9	23.9	21.8	18.4	13.7
Ismailia	8.1	9.1	11.0	13.6	17.3	20.2	22.2	22.5	20.7	17.8	13.9	10.0
Hurghada	9.6	9.9	12.3	16.1	20.7	23.5	24.8	25.0	23.2	19.7	15.5	11.9
Luxor	5.4	6.8	10.7	15.6	20.7	22.5	23.7	23.5	21.5	17.7	12.3	7.9
Aswan	9.5	10.6	14.0	15.2	23.5	25.1	26.1	25.4	24.0	21.7	16.5	13.2
Siwa	4.1	5.7	8.2	12.1	16.8	19.2	20.7	20.7	18.3	14.9	10.1	6.0
Kharga	6.0	7.5	12.4	14.8	17.6	23.1	22.3	22.9	22.3	18.2	12.2	8.3

MAXIMUM

MEAN MAXIMUM AIR TEMPERATURE °C

Town	Jan.	Feb.	Mar.	April	May	June	July	Aug.	Sept.	Oct.	Nov.	Dec.
Cairo	19.1	20.7	23.7	28.2	32.4	34.5	35.4	34.8	32.3	29.8	25.1	20.7
Alexandria	18.3	19.2	21.0	23.6	26.5	28.2	29.6	30.4	29.4	27.7	24.4	20.4
Mersa Matruh	18.1	18.9	20.3	22.7	25.5	27.8	29.2	29.9	28.7	27.0	23.4	19.7
Port-Said	18.0	18.7	20.2	22.6	25.8	28.5	30.4	30.9	29.2	27.4	24.0	19.9
Ismailia	20.3	21.7	23.9	27.6	32.1	34.8	36.4	36.5	33.9	30.7	26.7	21.5
Hurghada	20.6	20.9	23.0	26.0	29.6	31.4	32.6	33.0	30.6	28.5	25.7	22.4
Luxor	22.9	25.5	29.0	34.8	39.4	40.7	40.8	41.0	32.9	35.1	28.9	25.0
Aswan	24.2	26.5	30.6	35.6	40.3	41.9	41.9	40.6	41.0	37.5	31.4	26.5
Siwa	19.7	21.8	25.0	29.9	34.4	37.1	38.0	37.8	35.1	31.7	26.3	21.3
Kharga	22.5	25.0	29.9	31.4	36.0	41.1	39.9	39.9	37.6	32.6	26.6	24.6

The temperature drops sharply at night.

Clothes such as would be worn during spring weather in Europe and America are suitable for the Egyptian winter. A wool sweater or cardigan for men and women is a 'must' and a light coat will be useful at night.

During summer time only light clothes are needed – cottons, nylons etc. Low walking shoes are essential for sightseeing, preferably not the perforated kind because of sand.

A few small items can make all the difference during your visit. For instance on one trip along the Nile, I forgot my binoculars and, although other passengers were most generous in offering me theirs, I was loath to borrow because we always wanted them at the same time! As one of the delightful things about skimming along the Nile is watching the landscape, binoculars are most useful – and incidentally are one of the few things air travellers are allowed to carry about their person.

Sunglasses are helpful at any time of year and some sort of sunhat, although many tourists prefer to go bareheaded. Suntan oil is useful. Lipsalve is a good standby as lips are inclined to crack in a dry climate. A small torch is invaluable when visiting tombs and temples.

It goes without saying that a camera will be in your luggage. Lighting conditions in Egypt are ideal but films are expensive.

Should you forget anything in the way of dress there are excellent shops and most hotels have their own boutiques. Clothing and shoes are very reasonable in price.

Fishing is a popular pastime with tourists and locals alike. Wherever there is water there is fishing and Egyptian fishermen are most fascinating to watch. They ply their trade in the same way as the Disciples did on Lake Galilee. Little boats huddle together and lower their nets over the side. The boats bob up and down in the waves while the fishermen beat the water with sticks which makes a drumming, thudding noise. Apparently this frightens the fish below into the waiting nets.

Along the lake shores stand lone fishermen, knee deep in

water, whirling handnets above their heads and, with a deft rotating movement, casting them into the water in perfect circles. Edged with small weights, the nets plunge quickly to the bottom, ensnaring any fish in their path. One such net looks small from a distance but it is at least ten feet in diameter and is held by a long line suspended from the middle.

The lakes, the Suez Canal, the Red Sea and the Nile teem with fish of every kind; all Egyptians can enjoy this sport, whether it be with a bamboo rod costing a few piastres or expensive deep sea fishing equipment.

Epicures claim that fish caught in hot waters is tasteless. The reason is because the fish is not cooked soon enough. In a hot climate the full distinctive flavour can only be relished by cooking immediately after catching. There is no better way to ensure this than by fishing yourself and having a barbecue.

One of the seafood delicacies is soubia – small octopi. On dark moonless nights the Arab fishermen will entice these tiny creatures into special traps by shining torches over the side of the boat. A baby octopus is about two inches across. They are tiresome to prepare as they have to be skinned, a difficult job, then cooked for a considerable time in olive oil. The Egyptians excel in cooking soubia. It has a flavour all its own and often forms part of mezza the Egyptian equivalent of hors d'oeuvre.

The Egyptians use dough or live prawns as bait for rod fishing. Dough is made by kneading flour and water and adding a little cooking oil to bind it. The fisherman pulls bits off with his fingers, puts it in his mouth and after chewing it up into a little ball bites it on to his hook. I prefer the prawns. The knack of chewing the dough onto the hook I find difficult. It either disintegrates in my mouth or falls off the hook before I cast into the water.

The shores of the Red Sea offer excitement and adventure to skin divers. Sukhna is a favourite with underwater explorers. In some places glass bottomed boats are available for a top side view of the fantastic life in the coral reefs that, many say, have given the Red Sea its name. The most favourable months for big game fishing are September and October. At Hurgada

3. *Cairo: the East bank of the Nile with the Nile Hilton Hotel seen from the top of the Cairo Tower. Part of the Andalusian Gardens can be seen in the foreground*

and Sukhna there are modern hotels.

For centuries the Egyptian has had foreigners on his soil. In recent times tugs of war between the French and British and the occupation by the latter have caused much frustration to him. On the credit side he has become an excellent linguist and international in his thinking.

After the bloodless revolution of Nasser, Egypt reached a new era of independence. Now under the benevolent understanding leadership of President Sadat the Egypt of today is especially worth visiting. Nothing can explain this better than the statue in front of Cairo University, 'The Awakening of Egypt' by Mahmoud Mukhtar a modern Egyptian sculptor. Carved in granite, the material of the Egyptians of old, it is of a sphinx, symbolic of the pharaonic past. Beside it stands a figure, today's Egypt, raising her veil. She looks out over her own land and to the future with pride.

4. *Cairo: looking into the court of Sultan Hassan showing the Ablution Fountain*

2 Cairo

Cairo – the very name has an incantatory sound – although the oldest of cities is today very avant garde. The Nile, as always, is the main thoroughfare. Luxury air-conditioned hotels gaze at their startling white reflections. Skyscrapers creep upward on the margin of the river. Water buses skim the surface, trailing long lines of spray like glistening candy floss. Off one of the many islands a water spout, reminiscent of the one in Lake Geneva, gushes immense jets of sparkling water skyward. Cars dart gingerly amongst the buses and taxis which cross the many low-slung bridges – then verge off either side to the west bank or alongside the wide tree-lined corniche on the east. The best vantage point from which to see this astonishing city is from Cairo Tower. It soars some 600 feet into space and though made of reinforced concrete, has an attractive open lattice-work covering (twelve million pieces of pottery were used in the design) which looks deceptively fragile, especially at night when it is floodlit. It casts its long narrow shadow on the island of Gezirah, long known for its sporting club, the largest and most magnificent in the Middle East. The tower is encircled by a garden of its own where you will find chairs and tables for relaxing if you dislike heights. For those who wish to reach the top a handsome staircase of pink granite leads into the obelisk-like structure. The rounded walls of the entrance hall are studded with a series of mosaic pictures showing everyday life in modern Egypt. A speedy lift whisks you upward and in a matter of seconds you are higher than Cheops' Great Pyramid!

From the tower you can see that the city stretches from the

palm frilled Nile banks, across a wide plain, then sprawls in a thin line up the jagged slopes of the yellow Mokattam Hills. These rise above Cairo and act as a backdrop. To the far west, lush greenery, sliced into tiny squares by blue irrigation channels, ends abruptly in bone dry sand. Huddled in the desert lie the great tawny Pyramids of Giza.

Beyond the Giza Pyramids you can see the Step Pyramid at Sakkara. Far away in the distance a line of more pyramids looks like regimented toys against the horizon. Closer to hand there is the modern section of Cairo and the many faculty buildings of Cairo University. Eastward is the commercial centre with its high blocks of flats, shops and banks divided by tree lined streets.

It is said that even if a Moslem prayed in a different Mosque each day for a year he would not enter all the mosques of Cairo. Rounded minarets muse in the shadows of angular high buildings in the foreground and, farther off, crown the ancient parts of the city with semicircular crescents – the most lovely probably being the slender ones of the Alabaster Mosque known also as the Mohammed Ali Mosque.

Immediately below, at the base of the tower, the Nile flows north. Feluccas rest in the lee of bridges. Others, their lateen sails bellying in the breeze, glide along the water. The felucca, peculiar to Egyptian waters, has a single sail with a yard of astonishing length, so that it may catch each small gust of wind above the palm trees. A felucca looks as glamourous as a gondola – and is as easy to hire!

Views from the tower at night are quite different. The bridges spanning the Nile are lines of pale amber light, while from the heart of Cairo hectic neon signs pulsate on and off in flashes of colour. Those who have visited Cairo before will be astonished to find that the Mokattam Hills behind Saladin's famous Citadel, now has a road curling upwards in a series of lacets. On the very top is a casino with gaming rooms and a restaurant. There are several lookouts for motorists on the way, and for the first time you can look down on the high pencil thin minarets of the Mohammed Ali Mosque in the Citadel. The latter's history can be heard nightly when there is an impressive 'Son et Lumiere' performance. A frightful massacre took place there in the 1820s. Mohammed Ali resented the power of the Mamelukes. They were originally slaves who had gained their freedom and become similar to feudal barons and were a law unto themselves. He invited the leading ones to a banquet, commanded the gates shut and had them all killed. It is believed that one Mameluke leapt over the wall on his horse and the dreadful story spread quickly. One of the guides told me he was somewhat nonplussed when an elderly spinster in a group said in horrified tones, 'How thoughtless of Mohammed Ali to massacre them BEFORE the banquet!'

Cairo's Museum of Egyptian Antiquities houses some of the oldest relics in the world which include a unique collection of wondrously preserved mummies of different dynasties. These are in a special gallery and are well worth the few extra piastres you pay to enter. Yet inevitably the royal trappings of King Tutankhamen draw people like a magnet and there are those whose sole reason for visiting Egypt is to see them.

Crossing the threshold of the Tutankhamen Gallery you walk between two life size statues. Golden skirts encircle their loins, sandals of gold are on their feet and above proud foreheads they wear golden head-dresses. They stand at the alert, each man holding a staff topped with a golden ball. They flanked the sealed door that led to the burial chamber.

A handsome ebony life-size jackal, his ears cocked his golden collar taut about his neck, stares at the entrance. Despite his alertness his body lies in a horizontal position, haunches close to his side. He is the God Anubis, symbol of death.

All the trappings of court life are here, golden chariots, fabulous golden furniture, chairs, chests, divans, beds. Nowhere else in the world can so much gold be seen at once. Small golden figures displayed in glass cases depict scenes from the life of Tutankhamen in individual tableaux. Many portray dramatic incidents, such as the King about to harpoon a crocodile. Others represent happenings from the royal daily life. One glass case contains a gilden wooden shrine to Tutankhamen defended on each of its four sides by semi-nude guards, their arms outspread along the walls protectively.

Music was part of court life as can be seen by the slender trumpets and lutes. There are many perfume vessels of alabaster, one, a rounded jar, has a minute tiger as a handle, his small red tongue hanging out, his fur, tawny striped, looking so freshly painted it is impossible to believe it was carved some three thousand years ago.

The King's drinking cup is beautiful, made in a spherical shape from a single piece of the finest white alabaster. The bowl of the goblet is enfolded in a delicately carved lotus in full flower on a fluted base from which the handles spring in the form of lotus blossoms. The rim, perfectly round, is engraved with hieratic writing, inlaid with ebony, wishing the King longevity and good health. This goblet rests on a mirror so that it stands, narcissus-like, absorbed in its own perfection.

A terracotta bust of Tutankhamen, when but a boy, is balanced on a plinth in a small show case, while placed near a window is a sculptured stone head of the King at a later age. Both are quite perfect of feature but these are as nothing beside the famous golden mask. It is made of blue enamel, gold and lapis lazuli. The expression shows beneficence and tranquillity, unexpected in a face so young – for the King died at an early age. His jewellery is a sumptuous array of semi-precious gems, turquoise, lapis lazuli and cornelian. Long heavy ear rings lie beside necklaces and collars of elongated studded silver, scarabs, rings, anklets and bracelets.

At the end of the gallery there is the golden casket that encased the body of the Pharaoh. It had been enfolded by two outer gilded coffins which in turn lay in a huge stone sarcophagus. In another long glass case lies a golden replica of the King, gazing fixedly beyond the onlooker, his features as movingly beautiful as those of Nefertiti. The figure is clothed in gold, the folded hands hold the royal symbols of ancient Egypt, the whip and sceptre.

I have been fortunate in having visited the Museum on several occasions. One particular highlight was a few months ago when I watched scientists, headed by Dr. James Harris of Michigan University, X-ray several royal mummies. There was much excitement because no one in the past had dared unfold the final linen wrappings for fear of causing disintegration. Without actually touching the mummies at all, X rays would reveal what the shrouds had concealed for over 3000 years.

We waited while the cover was removed from the sarcophagus of the beautiful mother of Pharaoh Amenophis III, and X-ray equipment was swung gently over the exposed mummy. The head above the wrappings seemed only asleep. Rich honey coloured hair lay against the fine skull in waves. Unbelievably, in the electric light, the sheen remained as if the hair had just been brushed. Black eyelashes still adhered to the closed eyelids. It was impossible to think that this woman had lived thousands of years ago.

In turn other mummies received the same treatment and, later, the plates brought fascinating things to light. They showed priceless jewels embedded in the wrappings as well as tiny statues. At the feet of one princess, what was always believed to be a mummified baby turned out to be a baboon. Why this was so has not yet been ascertained. Perhaps the royal baby had not died and, to avoid it being murdered, a baboon had been substituted. Or, as a baboon was the animal associated with the moon goddess, there may have been some religious significance. Copies of the X rays have been placed next to the subjects for visitors to see.

Cairo is fortunate in having many other unusual museums. In the book 'Orientations' Sir Ronald Storrs relates how in the late 1920s he was one of the founders of the Coptic Museum cataloguing with Simaika Pasha, Vice-President of the Coptic Community Council, exquisite wool and linen weaving of the early Christian era, church vessels of copper, bronze and silver, manuscripts, ecclesiastical vestments and wood carving. He supervised the building of a traditional mud brick dome over one corner of an ancient church which was given the form of an old Coptic house, and incorporated ancient pillars, capitals and marble slabs in the structure. In 1931 it became a Government Museum.

Going through the Coptic Museum is like being shown over a magnificent mansion except for the wooden columns with placards in English, Arabic and French to explain the exhibits.

From earliest times Egypt exported textiles and cloth and in the museum you will see beautiful examples of tapestries and materials in wool and flax from the fourth, fifth and sixth centuries. (Silks were very rare in those days.) Young art students come to see them to get inspiration for making carpets and lace.

Ikons date from the fifth century and are all of religious themes. The Copts avoided representing scenes of the torture of saints and martyrs, the fear of the Day of Judgement or the Devil, so that the ikons have a pleasing gaiety and serenity. Originally the paintings were drawn directly on walls but by the eleventh century, because of persecution and flight, drawings were made on cloth, sheets of gold and ivory, so that they could be hidden in times of war or pillage.

Nearly every object is decorated with floral or fruit designs. Many plants had a special religious value such as the grape recalling that Christ said, 'I am the Vine'. This led to the use of vine branches, leaves and clusters of grapes embellishing capitals of columns, cornices and friezes. Palm fronds have been a sign since Pharaonic times of joy and welcome and are freely used.

Woodwork exhibits are beautifully carved. The Copts carried on the art from dynastic days and the Moslems carried on from the Copts. There are two amusing carvings, one called 'Petition of Rats' is of three rats before a cat, pleading for clemency and holding up a white flag. This was done between the fifth and sixth centuries. The other is a fresco of Adam and Eve eating the apple in the Garden of Eden.

In most of the vaulting frescoes Christ is the central figure and below Him in a semi circle is Mary with six disciples on either side. In one room there is a bronze Roman Eagle excavated from the south entrance to Babylon.

Coptic writing is similar to ancient Greek, only adding

seven letters from the 'fill in' sounds which were not found in the Greek. There are fine examples of Coptic writing on linen, wood and pot.

One of the latest museums to open is the Papyrus Institute which is just beyond the Sheraton Hotel and faces the Meridian Hotel on the opposite bank of the Nile. It is on board a houseboat and not only has examples of ancient manuscript but shows how papyrus was produced. You can buy sheets made today with attractive paintings by modern artists copied from ancient carvings. They range in price from a few pounds upward depending on the size and the paintings.

Some old houses have been opened to the public such as the 17th century one of Sheikh es Siahaimi and two antiquated houses joined together only by a top floor. This is a wonderful example of old Moslem architecture and was bought by a Mr. Gayer-Anderson some twenty years ago. It was built with direct access to the Mosque of Ibn Tulun. Gayer-Anderson lived there for some years and then bequeathed it to the nation for the most charming of reasons – in recognition of the years of happiness he had spent there. He died in 1942 and although since then the house has been a museum it still looks 'lived in' which adds to its fascination.

Gayer-Anderson was a great collector and furnished his house in different oriental styles. The main reception room has the middle part lower than the rest; this has a mosaic floor with a fountain in the centre, which your guide will put on for you if you wish. Jets of water fall over stone tortoises so that they seem to change colour like chameleons. The raised part of the floor is where the people sat. Mats would be placed on the stone floor in summer and warm carpets in winter. Of the windows, some are glazed or richly ornamented with stained glass, others have simply open lattice work or iron work. Those of the upper storeys are almost balconies and project out over the wall, being cased externally by the most beautiful mushrabia work. People within can see what is going on outside but are themselves entirely concealed from passers-by, or even the closest scrutiny from opposite neighbours.

The mosque next to this museum was built by Ahmed Ibn

Tulun, founder of the Tulunide dynasty who ruled Egypt from A.D. 870-904. He has been remembered for centuries because of his remarkable mosque which is said to be built over the spot where Abraham offered up the ram. It is a copy of the Ka'ba at Mecca and is believed to have been constructed by a Christian architect who was released from prison to carry out the work. The building is of the greatest interest architecturally for it shows that pointed arches were in existence well over five hundred years before their introduction into England. They are not of the later arabesque type but resemble a horse shoe design, inclining slightly inwards.

You enter the mosque by walking up a slope, going through some doors, up a further slope and then a short flight of steps, before getting into the mosque itself. At once you are aware of the quietness after the noisy street outside. The open court is square and stretches three hundred feet from side to side. On three sides it is surrounded by cloisters, consisting of two rows of columns. In the shadow, the tracery work of the window grilles rests against the blue of the sky and there is an atmosphere of calmness as you walk along the high cool colonnades and between the great piers. On the fourth side which faces Mecca, the aisles are five deep and in the centre of the court there is a domed fountain.

The minaret, the earliest in Cairo, rises beyond the walls of the mosque to the north west. It is charmingly simple in style, with a winding staircase outside leading to a gallery above. A story has it that Ibn Tulun was toying one day with a piece of paper and, twisting it round in a spiral, ordered that it be copied for the minaret.

The mosque of Sultan Hassan is regarded by many connoisseurs of Islamic art as the most beautiful mosque in the Middle East. The founder of this splendid building was the seventh of eight children of a ruling Mameluke Sultan. By a quirk of fate he was proclaimed Sultan after his father's death, at the early age of eight years. He grew into an intelligent young man but somehow caused the Regent such displeasure that he was imprisoned. However, he was released two years later and regained his throne. It was during the second part of his reign that the mosque was built, but before it could be completed Hassan met his death mysteriously in 1361.

The entrance is a most imposing portal, springing upward like a gothic arch, surrounded by honeycomb tracery and culminating in a shell design. Of the two minarets, the southern one is the loftiest in Cairo, soaring 267 feet into the sky. The open courtyard within the building is immense, with a richly decorated fountain in the centre. The dome over the mausoleum is 181 feet high, the highest in any Islamic monument. The iron chains which hang from the vaulting used to carry enamelled glass lamps, but these have been removed for safety to the Museum of Islamic Art. The mosque is rich in colourful ornamentation. The sculptured chair from which the Koran is read stands on eight slender pillars, a bronze door nearby is inlaid with damascene work in gold and silver and the richly carved *minbar* (pulpit) is of special interest to tourists. You are told that if you make a wish while walking beneath the great minbar it will be granted!

Opposite the Mosque of Sultan Hassan is the one of El Rifai near the Citadel and this is one of the most modern, having been completed only in 1910 by Khedive Abbas Pasha. Within its precincts are the tombs of the recent Kings of Egypt. Its handcarved minbar is studded with mother of pearl and ebony and the carpets are exquisite in colouring and design.

I shall not forget the first day I visited the mosque. The sun poured through the tracery design of a stained glass window in a diffused pool of light on a red carpet. Sitting cross-legged in the centre with head held high was an old, old man. Grey and black shawls were draped round thin straight shoulders. Beneath a snow white turban a thin wrinkled face looked heavenward, the almost black eyes calm, steadfast yet somehow expressionless, as if the man himself had ceased to exist and had become a statue. It typified age at its most venerable. Age when it has penetrated through the dross of life and is at peace awaiting the greatest experience man can know – death.

'How old is he?' I whispered.

'Of great age.'

'Over ninety?'

'Of course!' My guide looked so surprised I wished I had not asked. He continued, 'He is watcher of the dead here.' He strode over to the figure and whispered gently to it. The figure got to its feet in one straight movement. The old man was very thin and shrunken. One thin brown hand came out from under the draperies and held a large bunch of keys. We followed as he walked to a door which he unlocked. He stepped aside for us to go through, then pressed an electric switch.

Glass chandeliers flooded a high wall with light. In the middle towered a high sarcophagus. We felt dwarfed beside it as we examined the intricate carving with which it was covered. We entered a series of such halls each with a tomb, each with a different ornate design. If Arabic writing was above the tomb it meant that the person for whom it had been made was dead and the body in a vault below. If not, the owner was still alive. We were silent as the old man opened and locked each beautiful chamber of death. In one he turned the lights off for a few moments to enable us to admire the colour of the stained glass windows, through which the sun filtered.

When we returned to the main part of the mosque with its beautiful alabaster and ceramic walls, the old man motioned us to a hall with an exceedingly high vaulting. He sang out 'Allah' in a thin voice. The sound rang up along the walls, a paean of praise. We automatically looked aloft at the blue mosaic studded vaulting. 'Allah!' the old man's thin voice rang out once more. The echo followed us as we walked back to the main entrance. I hesitated and looked back over to the carpet where we had first seen the old man. He was sitting in the same place, but the sun had moved so he was in the dark. We left the Mosque El Rifai and stepped out into the bright sun of the Cairo streets.

An Arab historian asserts that Prince Aqsunqur for whom the 'Blue Mosque' was built in A.D. 1347 took such an interest in the project that he helped the masons in their work. His architect was given free rein with the design. Arches were raised on octagonal stone pillars and the narrow minaret is one of the most beautiful in the city.

Although the imposing columns are painted red and white, Robert Hichens, the English writer, named the lovely building the Blue Mosque and it has been known as that by visitors ever since. Once you go inside where walls are covered with the most charming delphinium blue faience tiles, you realize how the mosque got its new name. The tiles have enchanting motifs of cypresses and flowers but unfortunately some of them are missing. It is thought that during Napoleon's occupation his soldiers removed several pieces and sent them back to France. The blue walls and other appurtenances had been added by a Turkish governor after the mosque had been damaged by an earthquake.

Trees and shrubs grow by a pool in one of the open courtyards. This colourful mosque with its contrasting combination of Ottoman and Mameluke styles, the green of its garden, the red and white of the stonework, the differing blues of the pool, the sky and the faience tiles, although frowned upon by experts, is a great favourite of tourists.

The Citadel was constructed by Saladin in 1176 – historians claim that it was built with blocks of the smaller pyramids at Giza – and within its precincts there are three mosques, all beautiful and interesting but the one visitors remember best is the Mohammed Ali, which was designed by a Greek architect in 1824. It embraces two adjacent squares, one being the open courtyard fringed with domed porticos, the other the great praying hall in the form of a huge Byzantine dome, supported by four great columns and bordered by four semi-cupolas.

Built to resemble the famous blue mosque of Istanbul, it, like most famous buildings is alternately criticised and praised. It has been called too ornate, poor in design, too ostentatious to be in keeping with the Moslem tradition; or again, as one of the most magnificent of all mosques because of its large bronze windows, scores of lamps and fine mosaics. Before entering you pull large soft slippers over your shoes for the carpeting is exquisitely handworked. Once inside, you are immediately conscious of the tremendously high vaulting. Below it there is a vast emptiness, save for the tomb of Mohammed Ali. Underfoot the richness of the carpet stretches to the walls, which are of smooth honey and white alabaster. Overhead there are hundreds of globes electrically lit so that when they are switched on the mosque is flooded from the void above with subdued light, as if from many stars.

Leaving the mosque you can walk to the parapet on the ramparts to gaze over the city. In the late afternoon it is a hauntingly lovely sight. Cairo lies spread below the Citadel walls. In the background the Pyramids of Giza shimmer in the pink haze of the desert. Topped by thin crescent moons, signs of Islam, countless domes and minarets jut skyward from the huddled city. It seems a suitable place to end a day's sightseeing.

The site of the old Roman fortress of Babylon is the most ancient part of the city and is called Old Cairo. During the reign of Augustus it was the headquarters of one of the legions that garrisoned Egypt and parts of the Roman wall still remain. It is here that you will be able to visit some of the earliest churches in Christendom.

The 'Hanging Church' dates back to the third century and is built suspended between two bastions so that the entrance is up some twenty five marble steps and when you look out of the windows you see, not the ground, but down into a deep Roman moat – hence the name the Hanging Church. Having scaled the staircase you find yourself in a screened portico. Through a door in the back there is a small cloister and this leads into the church itself. On the right is a nine hundred year old painting of the Virgin and Child. The Virgin's eyes follow you as you walk from side to side. On the same wall there is an ikon of Saint Mark. One of the treasures is a carved wooden panel (from the tenth century) of the Nativity. The Holy Child is seen wrapped and laid in the manger, from which two animals are eating. The Virgin is sitting by the manger which is carved with Coptic crosses. The Coptic cross is like the Spanish and Maltese crosses, with three end points symbolising the Trinity.

I was taken over the Hanging Church by the Chief Priest, Shenouda Hanna. Against the third column in the central nave he pointed out the magnificent pulpit. It rests on fifteen delicate columns, seven pairs arranged behind a single one. Each pair is identical but no two pairs are alike. The pulpit probably dates from the twelfth century. In a wooden coffer close by are the bones of four saints.

The Baptistery is near the front entrance, the font being made of stone in commemoration of the rock from which water flowed miraculously by command of Moses in the desert. Baptism in the Coptic church is by total immersion. The wooden ceiling was remade some forty years ago, the wood being dovetailed together and shaped like a boat upside down.

The Reverend Hanna offered me a small circular sacrificial loaf of bread. As I hesitated, he laughed. 'It is not blessed,' he said. 'We have Holy Communion very early, extra bread is made but not consecrated, so that when the service is over the participants can eat it in lieu of breakfast.' The small loaf had the indentation of the Coptic Cross in the middle and twelve little ones around it, symbolising Christ and His twelve Apostles.

Saint Sergius' Church is unique in that the crypt is supposed to be the exact place where the Holy Family sheltered for a month after their flight to Egypt. Other parts of the church date back to the fifth century. The crypt measures some 20 feet by 15 feet and is bare save for some slender, marble pillars and a small recess. The church itself is small and oblong in shape and has three altars eastward, each in its own chapel. The pulpit is of rosewood inlaid with ebony and ivory. Another unique point about this church is that eleven of the columns in the nave are of streaked white marble and the twelfth is of red Aswan granite. Nothing is known about the saint after whom this church is named.

From Saint Sergius' Church you can go through a doorway in the garden and find yourself in a Jewish synagogue. It was once a Coptic church which was sold to the Jews by Michael, a patriarch towards the end of the ninth century. It is also small measuring only 65 feet by 35, but it contains some remarkable manuscripts one of which is said to be a copy of the Law written by Ezra.

The Church of Saint Barbara was built during the eighth century. It contains a small chapel to Saint George and has some delightful mural paintings. You will be shown a small receptacle which has a bone of Saint Barbara.

None of these Coptic churches has an organ. The only music allowed is by cymbals and brass bells. The latter are struck by a rod held in one hand. There are no images and paintings and ikons are in stiff Byzantine style, mostly portraying Christ in acts of benediction.

There are several Coptic legends, one of the most charming being that the Virgin Mary broke her fast when she arrived in Egypt by having a meal of dates. The cleft found in date stones is said to be the mark made by Mary's teeth.

About five miles to the north east of Cairo stands an aged sycamore tree called the Virgin's Tree. It was planted in 1672 from a shoot from another gnarled sycamore which was a place of pilgrimage during the fourteenth century. It was believed that beneath its shade Mary had rested with the Christ Child after crossing the desert. It was one of the things that the Empress Eugenie wished to see when she went to Egypt to open the Suez Canal and the Khedive Ismail presented it to her! Wisely, she left it where it was.

Not far from the Virgin's Tree you can visit the granite obelisk of Heliopolis. It was set up by Usertsen 1 in 2433 B.C. with a companion obelisk, both topped in copper and 66 feet high. They stood before one of the great temples in the rich city of On – Joseph married a daughter of Potiphar, a priest of On. Parts of the city were razed to the ground by the fury of Cambyses (the Greeks rechristened the city Heliopolis) and by 24 B.C. according to Stabo, it was in ruins. Arab writers say that many statues remained there in situ at the end of the twelfth century. The fabled Phoenix was supposed to be reborn there every five hundred years. Whatever the truth of the past all that remains now is the obelisk – but this is fascinating because it is the oldest in Egypt.

Cairo offers the choice of some of the finest hotels in the Middle East. The name first on everyone's lips is 'Shepheard's'. As long ago as the days of the Grand Tour rooms had to be booked there well in advance. Even then the hotel had a famous past. From its high ceilinged rooms General Gordon had set forth on his ill fated mission to Khartoum, Gautier to watch the opening of the Suez Canal, and Burton to England where he astonished the literary world with his controversial translation of The Thousand and One Nights.

For well over a century famous – and infamous – people have been coming and going at Shepheard's. It is not only one of the most renowned hotels in the world – it is an institution. It has been rebuilt, enlarged, burnt down and its actual site has been changed three times, yet the tradition of excellent service carries on and many of the staff have known no other life than Shepheard's – the 'Head Boy' in the front hall, resplendent in red and gold uniform, whose expressionless face misses little, has been with the Company for half a century.

The amicable chairman, Saad Assem, should he be passing through the lobby, has the same welcoming smile whether it be for the Begum Aga Khan or a little girl tourist returning from her first visit to the Pyramids. He has been with the Company for many years and Shepheard's is part of his life.

One of the many facilities offered by the hotel is temporary membership of Gezirah Sporting Club a short distance away. Ambitious plans are in hand to give Shepheard's a complete facelift by the same company, Southern Pacific Properties Ltd., who are designing the R'as el Hekma resort near Mersa Matruh. They are also going to develop some 20,000 acres as a tourist village, including hotels, in the region of the Pyramids.

1970 was the hundredth anniversary of one of the oldest hotels in the Middle East, Mena House, and also saw the birth of the newest at that time, the Sheraton, designed by Egypt's leading architect Ramzi Omar.

Despite the hundred years difference in their ages both

5. *Cairo: the tiny mosque of El Gyushi, from which the late Aga Khan's mausoleum is copied, looks towards the Mohammed Ali mosque*

hotels have a link in that their names are not those of their founders but are Pharaonic. Readers may be surprised to know that the word 'Sheraton' is connected by chance with ancient Egypt for it was the name of one of Pharaoh Akhnaten's daughters – 'Sher' meaning 'little' and 'aton' meaning 'sun'. The name 'Sheraton' is inscribed in hieroglyphics at the entrance to the new hotel. 'Mena' was the first pharaoh to amalgamate Upper and Lower Egypt and it was felt that this Pharaoh's name seemed appropriate for an hotel built on such a unique site – facing the Great Pyramid of Cheops. A further link was that an Egyptian postage stamp was issued picturing the two hotels together. Mena House is featured with the Pyramids rising behind it while the Sheraton is backed by the Nile. Beneath are the dates 1870 and 1970.

The Sheraton has an attractive lobby. An unusual double staircase climbs upwards its glass balustrades decorated with gold Pharaonic motifs. The carpeted steps have a design of open lotus blossoms. The 396 guest rooms – fully air-conditioned as is the whole building – have private bath and shower, TV, and balconies with a view over the Nile or out to the Pyramids.

Two floors have 'Presidential Suites' decorated in Louis XVI style. On the second floor there is a sun deck and a circular heated swimming pool. The Grand Ballroom has four adjacent meeting rooms reflecting the growing tendency towards conventions and meetings.

The dining room at the top of the hotel has sweeping vistas over the river to the heart of Cairo, Gezirah, tree lined avenues and the Andalusian Gardens. The decor is charming. Leather lined walls are tooled with gilt. Modern mushrabia screens are wrought with the same precision as those at the turn of the century. The bar, to one side of the dining area is sunk low so as not to hinder the views through the picture windows. It is called the 'Mushrabia Bar' and its handcarved latticework is exquisite. Fortunately in Egypt the price of craftsmanship of this high order remains within reasonable bounds even today.

Mena House was originally the Royal Lodge of Khedive Ismail who used it as a guest house for friends who wished to

6. *Montaza Palace at Alexandria stands in a park and faces out over the Mediterranean*

7. *A narrow strip of fertility often supports villages along the banks of the Nile like this one at the base of Gebel Selin cliffs*

visit the Great Pyramid and Sphinx. As the years went by it changed hands many times and, like Midas, it always attracted wealth and was enlarged extensively. When an English couple, the Locke-Kings, bought it they thought it might be fun to turn it into a luxury hotel. With plenty of money at their disposal they enlarged the mansion yet again and set about converting it into the quintessence of comfort but with fittings, architecture and decoration retaining oriental design. They gradually bought antiques from various towns in Egypt including screens and furniture of 'mushrabia' exquisitely cut wooden lattice work inlaid with ivory and mother of pearl. This ornamental furniture has been handled with such care during the last century that it is still used today. The chairs and couches, although fragile in appearance, are strong and fitted with cushions, which give the appearance of being upholstered. This ensures that the guest is comfortable and at the same time preserves the lovely workmanship.

In the eighties, at a time when hotel balconies and swimming pools were unheard of, each bedroom at Mena House had an open balcony leading from French windows so that guests could enjoy having their breakfast out of doors if they wished. The swimming pool, believed to be the first one in any hotel in the world, was a large marble one. To keep it spotlessly clean in the days before filtration, it was emptied each night and a line of servants would scrub the interior. It was refilled at dawn each morning.

Beneath the sandsweeps surrounding the vast Pyramids the hotel sprawled on its different levels, basking in the vivid sunlight through the years until the sunbaked walls seemed to merge into the desert itself. It fitted as naturally into the Pyramid complex as the Sphinx and became so famous that no one dreamt of visiting the Pyramids without at the same time having at least a cup of tea on its spacious terrace.

World renowned people have walked through its welcoming doors over the years. During 1943 plans for 'Overlord' – the invasion of Europe – were discussed there by Churchill and Roosevelt and arrangements were made for their meeting with

Stalin in Teheran. It was from Mena House one day after tea that Churchill took Roosevelt to see the Sphinx for the first time. Churchill wrote: 'Roosevelt and I gazed at her for some minutes in silence as the evening shadows fell. She told us nothing and maintained her inscrutable smile.'

Doctor Zaki Souidan is a doctor of international repute these days but during the second world war he had his first practice in Mena village close to the hotel. The head chef at Mena House was a patient of his. During the Churchill, Roosevelt and Chiang Kai-Shek conference, the chef was not feeling well and had to go to Doctor Souidan several times. One night he arrived with a large jar of caviar which he presented to the doctor. Zaki looked at it in surprise and asked where it came from. 'Well,' said the chef, 'Stalin sent three jars to Mena House for Mr. Churchill, and I thought two were enough for him.'

Many kings and queens have stayed at Mena House but none had a query answered·in the same way as the Duke of Edinburgh. He lunched at Mena House after visiting the Pyramids. The manager, who had welcomed so many famous personalities at the hotel, walked down the terrace steps to greet the Duke and suddenly was overcome with emotion. When the Duke made some laughing remark he replied, 'Yes Madame!'

To bring the Mena House story up to date I have to mention that a new hotel has been built called the Mena Garden Oberoi, in what used to be the gardens of the old one. It is operated by the Indian based Oberoi chain which has world wide connections. Ratan Tata is the general manager of their whole Middle East operation which also includes the Oberoi in Aswan and comfort and modernity are the watch words. Most exciting of all will be the complete refurbishing of the old Mena House to bring it up to international luxury standard. It is due to reopen early in 1976 and will combine the most up to date ideas and yet at the same time retain the priceless mushrabia work, moorish vaulting and irreplaceable furniture. The marble pool has already been replaced by a large modern one in which you can see the reflection of the

Great Pyramid as well as swim in its shadow.

Of the many other hotels in Cairo I must include the Meridian run by Air France and superbly sited on the Nile corniche so that from one side of the building you have the impression when looking out of the windows that you are aboard a great ship on the river. The view includes the Nile Hilton Hotel on the corniche far away on the right. This has 400 air-conditioned rooms. The main restaurant is built with two-level seating so that every guest may have a view of the river. The hotel decor has a Pharaonic flavour. As at Shepheard's there are self contained duplexes on the top floor. One of the Nile Hilton's specialities is cold meat suppers on Tuesday nights.

Some visitors still prefer the dragoman to the modern guide and the hall porter of any hotel can arrange for one to take you where you wish. Thomas Cook retain a few dragomen who have worked for them for years – and their fathers before them – and are extremely knowledgeable. Always dignified, they wear long robes and brocaded shawls and look as if they have stepped out of the pages of The Thousand and One Nights. They usually carry a walking stick – which can be used as a pointer when deciphering inscriptions!

I love the story of one who recently showed an annoying woman tourist around. She asked endless questions and did not wait for the answers. He was taking her back to the Nile Hilton Hotel where she was staying. She gazed at the Nile flowing by. 'What is the name of that river?' she asked. 'That is the Nile, lady,' said the dragoman patiently. 'What is it called after?' The dragoman looked pained then his eyes twinkled mischievously. 'It is named after the ˙Nile Hilton, lady!'

Nightclubs and discotheques are reasonable in price – it depends on what and how much you drink. Remember that Egyptian wines are extremely good and far cheaper than foreign ones. Most of the hotels have cabarets with oriental orchestras and belly dancers. If you would like to have an unusual night out you can go to Sahara City, a series of tents out beyond the Pyramids of Giza. The main one is a vast oriental marquee where you can dine, dance and watch a cabaret as long as a theatre revue. The cabaret includes Dervish dancers who are hypnotic to watch. They skilfully manipulate castanets and tambourines, make swooping movements towards the floor and at the same time whirl and spin continuously so that their stiff, heavily embroidered robes float out horizontally as if fixed in space.

If you do not want to have dinner on hotel rooftops and in fashionable nightclubs there are houseboats, such as the Omar Khayyam, moored on the Nile bank, where you can dine quietly and well. There are several espresso bars, cafes and ordinary restaurants. Both of the Groppi establishments are famous for their cakes and rose petal jam and serve the best ice cream sodas in Cairo.

One of the astonishing things about Egypt, which never fails to surprise me, is the quickness with which things happen. Several times I was driving along in a taxi when without warning a bunch of roses was held under my nose and a smiling face a few inches away said, 'Smell lady.' Before I could think, bouquet and man had vanished. All that was left was the scent of roses and a shot of adrenalin in the region of my stomach. I felt certain the man would be killed by an oncoming car and peered anxiously out of the window. My flower seller was dancing like Nureyev among the cars and taxis and others like him formed a corps de ballet. Flowers were waved overhead with elan. There were no accidents, no slackening of speed and, as far as I could see, few sales. The flower ballet dancers often have their roles taken over by newspaper sellers. The performance is similar. A newspaper is thrust into your taxi but before you can see if it is in Arabic, English or French, it disappears.

There are two newspapers in English, *The Egyptian Mail* and *The Egyptian Gazette*. The latter has been established since 1880. There are also booklets issued each week to hotels for visitors, called This Week in Cairo and This Week in Alexandria, which are in English and French and tell what is going on during the forthcoming week.

No holiday is complete without souvenir hunting and there

are some fascinating shops in Cairo – such as the Maison des Arts where there is a permanent exhibition and sale of Egyptian arts and crafts. It is near the Citadel and is an old Mameluke house of the sixteenth century. It also has an oriental tearoom. The main shopping centre (26th July Street and Talaat Harb Street are the most popular) has several department stores and little boutiques. In Shawarby Street you will find a mixture of goods from all over the world. It is far cheaper to have something made to measure than buy it off the peg! Hand made shoes are half the price paid in any other capital. Shop prices are controlled by the Government and are clearly marked so it is well worthwhile to learn Arabic numbers up to ten. (See elsewhere.)

But without doubt the most exciting place to go shopping is the famous Mousky and no visitor to Cairo can leave without several excursions there. The streets are unbelievably narrow, often roofed overhead, some lanes a bare two or three feet in width. The Mousky teems with buyers and sellers and beneath the noisy voices there is a constant frou frou of sound as people brush by each other.

Through the crowd the ubiquitous bread seller hawks his unleavened loaves of bread or sells semeen, crispy rolls coated with fine seeds and threaded like doughnuts on long sticks. Semeen is most delicious when cut in half and spread with butter and cream cheese. Vendors sell all kinds of food from sweetmeats to a form of caviare. Stalls are heaped high with household requisites, brightly coloured materials and clothing and everything displayed in a showy way to attract the passer-by. Men and women keep up a constant quick witted bargaining and, although there is little or no room, there is much flailing of arms.

Loiterers watch the brazier or the coppersmith. Fathers teach sons many trades and one sees small hands twist and turn, carving, polishing or moulding fine silver wire into brooches and bracelets.

The making of amber necklaces is fascinating. Chunks of amber are turned on a crude lathe operated by a boy to produce honey coloured beads smooth to the touch.

Mohammedans buy them, as Roman Catholics buy Rosaries, to hold and slip through their fingers as they whisper the various names of Allah.

Clacking his little brass cups together, this noise denoting his trade, the water seller walks by in his picturesque garb, his copper lemonade carrier glinting in the sun that filters down through frayed awnings.

Small frontless shops and stalls back onto larger stores, everything in such close conglomeration you never know if you will come upon some tawdry exhibit or something that will make you gasp with pleasure. The Egyptian perfumer is famed. He can blend a scent specially for you. Small phials of essences of flowers and other haunting fragrances are held under your nose. You are assured that each is more exotic than the last until you cannot make up your mind which essence you find most alluring.

You can watch the weavers at work interlacing threads of different textures into anything from woollen materials to the finest brocades. The fabric shops contain silks, piques, organdies, muslins, shantungs, chiffons, taffetas, chantilly laces, velvets and, most beautiful of all, Damascus brocades.

The best known one is ATLAS where you can have exquisite embroidered kaftans made within the week.

I shopped one day for a brocade to be made into an evening frock and found what I wanted in a tiny shop owned by a very old man. I looked at some delicate lames, narrowing my choice down to two different colours. It took a little time to decide between a pale green interwoven with gold thread, or a blue lame tissue frosted with silver. I finally decided on the latter and asked how many metres I would need. The old merchant looked very pained.

'Madam, this is all in one piece and cannot be judged by the metre,' so saying he spread the whole piece out on his counter for me to see. I bought it and we talked over our cups of coffee.

'Madam, before you leave I should like to show you my greatest possession.' He clapped his hands and a *safragi* (servant) fetched a roll covered with tissue paper. The old man unrolled it reverently to display a multi coloured brocade intricately woven with real gold. The raised pattern of gold diffused the pastel shades so that they melted into each other. 'I have had it a long time,' he said gently. 'I wish I did not have to part with it but a man must do business. I shall hate to see it go. Feel it lady, it is as fine as the petals of a flower. Yet it is as strong as natural silk.' I felt the lovely stuff. The old man refurled the material with gentle hands. 'I can always afford to have one such piece in my shop, Madam. *El hamdo lel'Lah.*'

Uncut gems are to be seen at any Mousky jeweller. You will be shown small packets of sapphires, rubies and diamonds. Choice of cut depends on the strength of the stone and the strain it can sustain, so do not be too enamoured of a gem in its uncut state. Perhaps the best buys are the semi precious stones where there is not so much money at stake. You will be shown zircons with their flashing blues, blue greens or red browns, opals with their rich varied tints, amethysts, tawny topazes, garnets and the brittle colourful tourmalines.

Of the real gems emeralds seem to vary most in price. All are lovely from the lustrous dark greens (which are the most costly) to the pale coloured ones. When diamonds, rubies and sapphires were unknown, emeralds were highly prized in Pharaonic Egypt. Among jewels in the tombs of the Princesses Ita and Khumit (who were embalmed over 4000 years ago) a bronze dagger was found studded with emeralds and, amongst the jewellery with the usual cornelian and lapis lazuli, was a necklace with a clasp of emeralds and a strand of emerald beads.

The silver filigree work is very cheap, but very pretty. The tracery patterns look fragile but are deceptively strong. Filigree casings of silver and gold enfold charming little scent bottles with jewelled tops.

The most famous part of the Mousky is the Khan Khalili where there are innumerable gifts to take home and merchants make you welcome with the inevitable cup of coffee. Galabia material, a thick cotton which looks like heavy silk, can be bought in dress lengths. Silver is sold by weight, not by workmanship so that it tends to be cheaper. At Agati the silversmith's shop, you can buy traditional work and silver ashtrays which are made from anklets with little bells on them, bon bon dishes and all kinds of silver jewellery. The lovely pairs of birds and animals that have made their reappearance on European dining tables in recent years, are half the price of those in Paris and London. Mr. Agati is a member of the fourth generation to carry on the silver shop and has diplomas from France and Belgium.

Not far across the lane from Agati is Onnig, renowned for his jewellery designs. Onnig Alixanian is also a fourth generation merchant in the Mousky. He is a member of the American Gemmological Association and several pieces of his Pharaonic jewellery can be seen at the United Nations building in New York or the British Museum in London.

I asked Onnig about a beautiful necklace he had on display in the Khan Khalili. It was made of antique turquoise beads hung with amulets of gods and goddesses. The little amulets were encased in gold and had taken four years to collect. 'Gone are the old days,' Onnig smiled at me. 'Only 20 years ago the fallaheen would bring me in quantities of these – now they are becoming very scarce.' I asked what stones were indigenous to Egypt. 'Only two,' was the reply, 'turquoise and peridot. Turquoise from the desert and peridots from Saint John's Isle in the Red Sea, but they are becoming rare.' I was shown a brooch made in a design of these stones. The gem is a type of chrysolite, emerald green in colour. Onnig makes charming souvenirs to take home; cuff links and cartouche brooches in silver and gold, key rings, ashtrays and so on. His newest shop, known as Onnig's Cairo Museum Gift Shop, is to be in the main entrance of the Museum of Egyptian Antiquities. Here he will sell copies of Pharaonic jewellery and small Pharaonic models.

Although the merchants in the Khan Khalili are invariably male, women own various boutiques in the ordinary shopping centres. Indeed, despite the fact that the number of Egyptian women holding key positions is still small, modern education has opened all fields of work to them. It may make our women's liberation movement jealous to hear that, ever since their emancipation, women have received equal pay with men in government jobs. Women are engaged in scientific research, medicine and can become members of parliament. In the arts women have always played their part. Who can forget the mass grief when mourners attended the funeral of Um Kalsum, the singer who enchanted not only Egypt but the whole of the Middle East, with her marvellous voice. It had such sway over the Arabs that both the Germans and the British used her records during the last war in their Arabic programmes. Wealthy oil sheiks chartered aeroplanes to come to her concerts which were always held on the first Thursday of the month. Her records are cherished and can still be heard on the radio almost daily. When a hyperthyroid condition endangered her voice in 1954 she was invited to Washington for treatment. A vast crowd wished her bon voyage at Cairo airport and medical bulletins were issued daily in Egypt about her progress. When she returned home, cured, her followers went mad with delight. Her voice was still magnificent and a saying grew up that two things never changed in Egypt – the voice of Um Kalsum and the Pyramids.

I was fortunate enough to be invited to her villa one day and found her to be small in stature and, although proclaimed to be one of the richest women in the world with a wonderful jewellery collection, she received her guests that day in an austere cream and pale green salon sparsely furnished. She wore a simple well cut black dress unadorned save for a peerless string of creamy pearls.

By chance Um Kalsum read her own obituary notices and was delighted with them. She was in a coma in hospital and the word went around that she had died. The papers next day were grief stricken. However Um Kalsum rallied and asked to see the papers with her morning tea. Unfortunately she weakened during the day and within a short time she died. Her funeral was led by the chief of the presidential court who deputised for President Sadat. The mile long procession included ministers, musicians, film stars, poets and thousands of her followers who chanted – 'Farewell, farewell our beloved lyre.' She had come from the fellaheen and they adored her and she them. Later it was found out that during her lifetime she had looked after some 200 fellaheen families.

Egyptians love music and perhaps this gives them their facility for languages. Samira Abdel Sayed was one of the first women to become a simultaneous translator and now attends international conferences and discussions at the UN headquarters in New York and OAU meetings. She has acted in plays on television and radio and also has a weekly programme on Cairo radio called 'Radio Guest' where she interviews visiting personalities.

A schoolfriend of Samira's, Siham Raouf, is just as versatile. When you meet this pretty, chic young woman, her fingers covered with rings in the prevailing fashion, you would never guess that she is general manager of passenger flight services for Egypt Air and is also responsible for the catering and food supplies for most of the foreign carriers at Cairo Airport. She is the only woman member of the Arab Carrier Catering Committee and its first chairman. She was awarded the State Merit prize first class in 1968 for business efficiency, ingenuity, and production – the first woman to receive it.

Before I stop eulogising about the modern Egyptian woman I must mention Madame Sadat. When I was presented to her at a YWCA bazaar I noticed that her English was faultless, that she is very soignee and pretty with blonde hair. She was interested in all the stalls and when she left every women in the hall felt better for her presence. 'She is just what one imagines a President's wife should be,' remarked one lady.

One of the oldest traditions in Egypt is hospitality. Egyptians love receiving guests and often even on the telephone one of their first greetings to one of their own family or perhaps someone they have only seen the day before is 'Welcome, twice welcome.' '*Ahlen-wiz-ahlen.*' Nowhere will you find this more apparent than when you fly Air Egypt. The airline was formed in 1928 and today their Horus head motif is carried by an all Boeing fleet. It has regular services from London to Cairo, some nonstop and in just over five hours from Heathrow you can be landing in Cairo. British Airways also provide services to Cairo. It is often as difficult to get seats on this route as it is to find hotel accommodation on arrival.

The capacity of both airlines will undoubtedly be increased in coordination shortly for demand grows.

Thomas Cook, whose founder opened an office in Cairo at Shepheard's in 1873, are now building their own hotel at Bulac where the old port of Cairo used to be. The company has been associated with travel in Egypt since before the opening of the Suez Canal. Incidentally Cook was the first person to invent the return ticket and 'Hotel Accommodation Coupons' and the company still use the word 'coupon' for their cable address.

One of the farseeing Egyptians in tourism management and marketing is Dr Salah Abdel-Wahab. A few years ago Director General of Tourism in Egypt he is now Professor of Tourism at the International study centre in Turin. Though resident there he visits Egypt frequently and serves on President Sadat's National Council on Productivity and Economic Affairs. A fellow member is the brilliant financier Mohammed el Kaissouni who is President of both the International Arab Bank and the European-Middle East Banking Group and involved in the provision of new luxury hotels. With men of this calibre and the sunny dry climate – surely tourism's greatest asset – the needs of visitors will be well catered for in the future.

At the beginning of the century Heliopolis was developed on some five thousand acres north of Cairo with broad streets, parks and clubs. It now merges into the city and is Cairo's most prosperous suburb. Some fifteen miles to the south lies Helwan, Egypt's pleasant little spa. It is entering upon another wave of popularity such as it has enjoyed at many times through its eventful history, which goes back thousands of years.

It was a renowned health resort in predynastic times which excavations have proved. Its Arabic name was given by a brother of the Caliph Abdel Malek who settled there during an epidemic of plague which spread through Cairo in the middle ages.

Khedive Ismail made his winter residence at Helwan. The exiled Turkish artistocracy (who had fled from the despotism of Sultan Abdul Hamid) followed his example. By 1899 palaces and beautiful villas had made their appearance and the Khedive inaugurated a large building for thermal baths.

Then, during the trials of The First World War, the international vogue of staying at Helwan disappeared. Little by little the once fashionable resort faded and was not fully resuscitated by the time the 1939 war swept over the world.

Now, once again, Helwan has been aroused from her sleep. The Sulphur Baths establishment caters for rheumatic patients and is well equipped with the most up to date scientific appliances.

A short distance from the baths are the mineral springs. Only a few years ago a new spring erupted similar to waters from Vichy and Monte Catini.

Perhaps the most delightful thing about the Egyptian climate is that you can plan ahead to go on an outdoor picnic on any special occasion. You can spend days going to the outskirts of Cairo on intriguing excursions, say to Memphis or Sakkara.

At Memphis you can see a gigantic recumbent figure of Ramses 11. Over it has been built a new open air gallery, thus stopping tourists clambering around the statue and enabling those with cameras to get pictures from various vantage points. From there it is but a step to see an eighteenth dynasty alabaster sphinx which is erected exactly over the place of its excavation.

At Sakkara there is the amazing Step Pyramid of King Toser, created by an architect Imhotep about 2770 B.C. Its sides do not exactly face the cardinal points and in shape the pyramid is oblong. Of the many pyramids in Egypt this one is particularly impressive in the evening when its six great steps stand out against the darkening sky.

The tomb of Ti, with its detailed charm is certainly the most beautiful one at Sakkara, with its exquisite carvings. Ti was a young, handsome noble (you can see his statue in the Cairo Museum) and very rich, to judge by the wall reliefs. On the north wall he is in a boat going through a papyrus thicket close to the bank where you can see fledglings being fed by a parent bird in their nest. Other birds are sitting on their eggs. In a boat preceding Ti's, boatmen are trying to harpoon hippopotami. A baby hippopotamus is trying to climb on its mother's back, another is biting a crocodile. From Ti's boat his steersman is fishing. It is a carving full of action, yet at the same time peaceful. The other murals are equally delightful and I must mention one. It is on the south wall and shows Ti and his lovely wife, Neferhotpes, watching animals being brought before them which will later be sacrificed in the temple. Cattle are wearing ceremonial collars and being led by leather leads, antelopes are being held by their antlers. Before Ti stands his steward checking an inventory papyrus scroll.

Also at Sakkara are the vast corridors of the Serapeum where the Apis bulls — elaborately worshipped during their lifetime – used to be laid to rest in mummified splendour.

The name Ti is sometimes pronounced 'Tie' sometimes 'Tea'. There is a story of an elderly lady tourist who after she emerged from the Serapeum was told that they were going to the 'Tomb of Ti'. She exclaimed with delight: 'Oh! how lovely, I could just do with a cup!'

This story is only equalled at Sakkara by Sir Ronald Storrs who lost four of his party of seven when he was leading them around the Sakkara sights and finally discovered they were enjoying a quiet game of bridge on a fifth dynasty sarcophagus!

I cannot revisit Sakkara without memories of Professor Walter Bryan Emery who in recent times was Britain's most famous Egyptologist. For over forty years he spent half of each year in Egypt, much of it at Sakkara pursuing his life's ambition to find the tomb of Imhotep. It was almost a religious dedication.

The looming six step pyramid was built by Imhotep for Pharaoh Zoser and Bryan Emery was convinced the former's tomb must be close by. Imhotep had been a great statesman and a doctor of exceptional skill. He became known as the 'great healer' and after his death was worshipped as a god in a shrine some distance from the necropolis. With blue eyes glittering behind his spectacles Bryan used to tell of his discovery of a slab with hieroglyphic inscriptions reading: 'To Imhotep the Great, Son of God Ptah and other Gods who rest here.' In his search Bryan Emery found countless lovely things and gallery after gallery was unearthed containing hundreds of ibis mummies. I visited this underground labyrinth with him one day and he showed me an ibis mummy he had found the day before. It was wrapped in linen and had an intricate gold insignia on the top. According to theology the ibis was sacred to the ancients and identified with Imhotep. Like Sherlock Holmes Bryan would say with certainty 'In the labyrinths and their contents I have my clues. We are on the right track.'

During the discussion over moving the Abu Simbel monuments Bryan was excavating at Buhen in Nubia and supervised the dismantling of the lovely Hatshepsut temple there. It was to be in the grounds of the museum in Khartum and was a staggering operation at the time but he was not daunted by it. Stone blocks weighing as much as four tons were carried to the banks of the Nile, moved by barge to Wadi Halfa and then by rail to Khartum for re-erection. Before this rescue operation he had made striking discoveries in excavations of the tumuli at Ballana and Qustol. But his quest for Imhotep was always foremost in his mind and he was soon back at Sakkara at his dig or working away in a low building known always as 'Emery's House'. He was happiest there, as was his wife Mollie who went with him everywhere. She took the everyday problems off his shoulders, catering for the helpers and reminding him about his visitors for he was the typical absent minded professor. He once took a governor over one of the sites and, as Mollie was not at his side, forgot his name. He did recall one name associated with the man and asked his guest how that gentleman was. 'I am perfectly well as you can see,' was the indignant reply. The story that he told me which I love best took place during the last world war.

Bryan served with the army and later became an attaché at the British Embassy in Cairo. He awoke one night suddenly and thought to himself that it would be a crime if a bomb fell on the Egyptian Museum of Antiquities and destroyed the mummies of the royal pharaohs. The next morning he busied himself trying to see if he could get them moved but no one was interested. He then went to a wealthy pasha on the outskirts of Cairo and asked if it were possible to have some of the mummies moved to safety into the pasha's mausoleum which had recently been completed. The pasha agreed. Bryan then had to think of a way to get them there. People kept pointing out there was a war on. Petrol could not be used for such an expedition. Bryan had an army doctor friend and persuaded him to lend him a few ambulances. Both men thought it advisable not to report what they were about to do or carry out their plan in daylight. On one moonless night several soldiers with stretchers carefully removed the precious mummies amongst them Seti 1, to their ambulances and drove them to the pasha's mausoleum. There they remained until after the war.

The last time I saw Bryan was in 1971. My husband and I bumped into him at the Semiramis Hotel (recently demolished to make way for a new larger one with the same name). He was pleased to see us and as happy as a schoolboy. He joined us for lunch. I asked why he looked so gay. He had at last found Imhotep? 'Where oh where is Imhotep?' he asked. 'We shall find him later. I am happy today because yesterday I found a delightful little statue of Horus, each feather a beauty and the head perfect.'

A few weeks later in England we read in the papers of his death after a stroke. His many friends were heartbroken especially the workers on his Sakkara dig who regarded him as a father figure. His will requested that he would be buried in Egypt. Recently Dr. Zaki Souidan took me to visit the grave in the British Cemetery in Old Cairo. Some people felt that he should have a special memorial over his grave but it is marked with a plain headstone with the words 'In loving memory' and recording the dates of his birth and death. I am sure that he would have wished for just such a simple resting place in the sands of Egypt which he loved so well, and where he spent so much of his life.

8. *Sunset at Aswan*
9. *Dervish dancing*

The search for Imhotep is continued by Dr. Geoffrey Martin and Dr. Ali El Khouli the chief inspector at Sakkara who both worked with Bryan for several seasons. When they set out from Emery's house each morning they never know what the day will bring. Like Bryan they search for clues and trust they are on the right track.

A regular visitor to Bryan Emery in hospital just before he died was Kamel el Mallakh. Egyptologists are an individual race as unlike in character as artists. Bryan shied away from strangers, Kamal is gregarious. Although both men wrote books, Bryan found it difficult to convey excitement, Kamal does not. Bryan was married, Kamal a bachelor. Bryan did not realise his life's ambition and Kamal accomplished his almost by chance.

A most gifted Egyptian, Kamal el Mallakh is modest by nature but enthusiastic about his many interests. He is on the staff of Cairo's *Al Ahram* and his articles, always on the back page, tell of the latest archaeological discoveries or are interviews with artists, writers and controversial people in the art world. His style is witty and crisp. He is invariably writing several books at once. For instance while writing a book on German music – he knows most of the scores of Beethoven, Chopin and Brahms – he was also engaged on another one called 'The Royal Mountain' on finds in the Valley of the Kings. Kamal trained as an architect and later took a PhD in archaeology. Egyptology is his great love. For several years he was Director of Works in the Giza Pyramid area.

I could not discover how Kamal could fit so much into 24 hours until I spoke to him about a tea party he had not attended. We were sitting at a table in Mena House garden at the foot of the Great Pyramid and I was watching two little hoopoes sweeping along the grass, their colourful plumage vivid against the green. Kamal put his coffee cup carefully in his saucer.

'I had been told you were coming to this tea party,' I said, 'but I did not see you.'

'I was coming but before I left my flat someone arrived with a document about Brahms that I had wanted for some time. It

10. Nile landing stage at the Cataract Hotel, Aswan

was far more important for me to read the document.'

'Do you often ignore invitations that you have already accepted,' I asked amused.

'Of course,' he replied simply, 'you must put important things first.'

'What happens if one of your friends gets upset because you do not keep an appointment?'

'If they do not understand, they are not real friends. Life is so short that if you do not write just when you feel like it, you may miss that inspiration for ever. If during excavations you stop just when people suggest a meal you would never get anything done.'

On the other hand Kamal is a stickler for time when it is anything to do with his articles for *Al Ahram,* which is Arabic for 'The Pyramid'. While he was working at Giza if a colleague suggested meeting him at *Al Ahram* he would ask 'Paper or Stone?'

Unlike most men Kamal has no interest in motor cars. He has never made time to learn to drive and has no wish to do so. A few years ago he had an old car and an aged driver – the latter because he did not like to be driven over 20 miles an hour – but when the driver died and the car fell to pieces he replaced neither. Kamal has no interest in money. When he made his discovery of the Pharaonic Solar Boat in 1954 near the Great Pyramid, cables arrived with offers for exclusive rights of the story. Kamal ignored them saying simply, 'God has been kind to me and the story is for everybody.'

Kamal took me to see his discovery. The beautiful boat had been constructed to take Cheop's soul to everlasting life along the river Tuat bridging life and death. A museum has been erected over it between the Pyramids of Cheops and Chephren.

What Cheops mighty Pyramid was to do for the Pharaoh's body, the boat was to do for his Ka, his soul.

It is most beautiful and stretches almost 150 feet in length, some of the timbers being made from whole cedars of Lebanon. Bow and stern alike are shaped in graceful sweeping curves topped with carved papyrus blossoms. There are dark brown wooden oars, flat and smooth. The boat's state of preservation is remarkable. It is the most fantastic find since Tutankhamen's tomb. The story of the Solar Boat's discovery is scarcely less fascinating than the find itself.

In April, 1950, close by the side of the Great Pyramid which faces the Sphinx, a road was being made for the convenience of tourists. Kamal was asked to keep an eye on the digging. His excitement was great when his men dug down to limestone powder – not the kind that capped Chephren's pyramid close by but of the type found in the Mokattam Hills on the other side of Cairo. As the men continued to dig they came upon a pinkish cement which sealed together great slabs. Was this a large flat base or a great roof? Kamal was of the latter opinion, but it was difficult to be sure and often great finds seem imminent only to end in disappointment. Perhaps the slabs formed part of the foundation of Cheop's pyramid. Kamal had been working on the Giza site for some years and it was the first time he felt Cheops' Solar Boat might be uncovered. The area was in the exact position that Cheops, on the law of averages, would have chosen. But boat pits by the lesser pyramid had yielded nothing and, even if it was a boat, it might have been robbed in antiquity. Kamal felt he would be satisfied if only some vestiges of a Solar Boat were found. All boat pits could not be empty. Of one thing he was certain. He could not rest until he knew the answer.

Together with the team of men he cleared an area large enough to see that the great slabs might indeed form a roof. He then began to scrape down between two blocks which seemed less sturdy than the others. He made a deep chink between the two. On 26 May 1954 he began digging in earnest. He kept on until the hole was large enough for him to be lowered into it head first. He was armed with cutting and probing instruments and continued scraping.

He paused for a time and glanced up along his body to the sky above him and could see a black shadow lying along the apex of Cheops Pyramid. Yet he could see no clouds. The sky was the colour of lapis lazuli. He felt it was a momentous occasion and for this reason his heart flailed against his rib cage.

He closed his eyes to accustom them to the gloom of his digging then opened them slowly. With a steady hand he began to cut again. He worked quickly as the casing gave way and crumbled. He made the hole deep enough to twist his body in a different position downward and working only a few inches away from his head he kept on cutting and cutting. Time meant nothing. He was not conscious of his tiredness or of lying in a perpendicular position. He probed. He cut. Suddenly and miraculously his hands went through into nothingness. He lay as if in a trance. An almost imperceptible smell crept into his nostrils. He could not define what it was. It was almost sweet. It could not be incense. Or was it? Was it perhaps the very smell of history? Then he knew. It was cedar wood! His eyes were still unopened. He drew a deep breath down into his lungs. It was indeed cedar wood. He felt a sense of fulfilment such as he had never known before. Happiness tingled through him. His eyes were still closed. He whispered a prayer of thanks to God. His questioning mind began to function again. If indeed he smelt cedar wood from a Solar Boat below it did not mean that the white ant had not been busy. Perhaps the precious wood had been eaten through by hordes of them.

He shouted up to his men to hand him down his mirror. It was a small, shaving one. He reached up with one arm as far as he could and the mirror was lowered to him. He brought his hand down gently and gradually twisted into a new position so that he could plunge his arm down as far as possible into the aperture. The smell of cedar wood was now unmistakable but he could see nothing. He pushed his head against the jagged stonework and tried to turn his body so that the sunlight would slant down his back into the opening. He rocked his hand to and fro. Suddenly he caught sunrays on the mirror. He manipulated it slowly so that the light reflected downward. He saw something – something bright. What could it be?

He carefully moved the mirror once more and then he

suddenly saw the tip of an oar. His hand began to shake. He felt a great strength surge through his whole body.

'It is the boat.' he shouted. 'It is the boat!'

Willing trembling hands pulled him upward. His men were beside themselves with joy. '*Mabrouk! Mabrouk!*' (Congratulations, congratulations) they cried, tears streaming down their faces.

Kamal held his hand to his forehead. It was shaking and his forehead felt hot and sticky. He looked at his palm. It was covered in blood. 'Your head! Your poor head,' said one man holding a handkerchief solicitously. Kamal had shoved his head so far into the stone that he had gashed his forehead deeply without knowing or feeling any pain.

As Kamal finished telling me the tale of how he had found Cheops' Solar Boat in its pit, I looked at his forehead. An indented white mark showed up against his tanned skin.

'I suppose one might call it an honourable scar,' he smiled.

3 Alexandria

If you arrive in Alexandria by sea, even before you dock your eyes will be drawn to an enormous, white dome-shaped three-storeyed building. As you come closer you will notice that its length stretches five quays. It is the Maritime Station. Once moored, your ship is linked to the station building by electrically-controlled gangplanks and you are shown directly into a beautifully proportioned hall. It is a large place with mosaic murals on the walls. Here you will find a tourist information bureau, banks, post and telegraph offices, waiting rooms, tourist agencies, shipping lines, a restaurant and a cafeteria. There is an excellent shopping centre where you can not only buy things and get an idea about prices, but can have them shipped home. It is also a good place to spend your remaining holiday money before returning to your ship.

A bridge which cost some E£34,000, leads from this modern building over the docks to the main exit (all formalities for landing are arranged before you leave your ship) and everything that will facilitate a tourist's arrival has been foreseen. Special buses are waiting. A train which goes straight to Cairo as soon as all passengers are aboard, waits in the station.

Should you visit Alexandria by car from Cairo it is about 160 miles distant along what is called the agricultural road which is an interesting one through the Delta via Benha, Tanta and Damanhur. Part of it is a four lane highway divided by shrubs and greenery down the centre and edged with canals which are often wide enough for feluccas. There are one or two cafes on the way. You can also drive along what is called the Desert Road, which is the bus route. The train journey from Cairo is another alternative. Frequent diesel services make the journey in less than three hours.

Should you arrive in Alexandria by air from Cairo, you see the city from another angle. Instead of the vastness of the harbour and maritime building you land at a small, tidy airport surrounded by formal gardens. Alexandrian taxis are orange in colour with black mudguards. One of these can take you through the city to your hotel. The route is attractive, passing by Nuzha public park with its gardens and zoo and then through the university quarter with its various faculties.

Situated on the southern coast of the Mediterranean, Alexandria enjoys a mild temperature in winter and a moderate one in summer. Sherif Street, which is the main one, has branches of some of Cairo's largest shops such as Salon Vert, where the ground floor is full of all kinds of materials somewhat cheaper than in the capital because Alexandria is the home of the best cotton in the world. Here for less than £2 a metre you can buy linen, cotton jersey, voile, gaberdine, and other cotton weaves in lovely designs and pure silk at less cost than in Europe or America. The best known antique shop, Habashi, is also in this street and many shops where you can buy leather goods, and order handmade shoes which are too reasonable in price to resist. I asked Nadia Ibrahim, the local director of Tourism what were the most popular buys for visitors and without hesitation she said, 'Everyone thinks cotton of course but in fact leather shoes and handbags are the best sellers, followed by rugs and cotton comes third. After these three it is difficult to say but kaftans for both men and women are popular.'

Sherif Street goes straight through the town parallel to the corniche – which is about 15 miles (25 kms) long. The western harbour is for shipping, the eastern harbour for yachting and fishing.

Alexandria, one of the most famous cities of antiquity, was founded by Alexander the Great in 332 B.C. It lay on a narrow strip of land separating Lake Mareotis from the Mediterranean. Two splendid harbours were formed by a small rocky island, called Pharos, being joined to the land by a mole nearly a mile long. On the north east corner of Pharos towered a 600-foot white marble lighthouse, one of the seven wonders of the world and the model from which the world's lighthouses were to be copied.

Alexandria was a great trading centre under the Ptolemies with a mixed population of Egyptians, Romans, Jews and Greeks. A special feature was the underground tank system which held more than a year's supply of water. Rhacotis was the Egyptian quarter where stood the Serapeum and the Pillar of Pompey. The royal palaces were at the east end of the city together with the famous Alexandrian library with its wealth of ancient literature.

The world owes much to Alexandrian scholars, Euclid the geometrician, Hipparchus the astronomer and Ptolemy and Eratosthenes the geographers. The library contained priceless manuscripts and those who studied there included Strabo (from whom we learn much about ancient Egypt) and Archimedes, the Greek mathematician, whose method of irrigation, raising water by tube in the form of a screw wound round a cylinder, is still used in Egypt today.

When during the time of Julius Caesar the library was burnt down more than 750,000 works were lost. Later Antony handed some 200,000 manuscripts over to Cleopatra and these became the foundation of a second library. The name Alexandria is always inextricably associated with that of Cleopatra, for it was there that she knew Caesar and was crowned. It was there, on the site now known as Ar-Raml Square, that she built a temple for Antony, the entrance to which she adorned with two obelisks brought from Heliopolis that had been made during the reign of Thothmes 111. Today one is on the Thames Embankment, Cleopatra's needle, the other is in New York in Central Park. Cleopatra's library fared no better than the one before it. In A.D. 641 at the command of the Caliph Omar, the manuscripts were destroyed. He is supposed to have said that if they held the same doctrine as the Koran they would be useless as the Koran contained all necessary truths. If they included anything contrary to the Holy Book they ought to be destroyed, so in either case they must be burnt. Legend has it that these were used as fuel to heat the public baths – lasting for six months!

During the fourteenth century successive earthquakes and a gigantic tidal wave demolished the city. All traces of the wonderful lighthouse vanished. Not only had its high brazier of fire guided the ships into harbour but it had housed a large garrison in its three hundred rooms. Gone was its vast mirror of legendary fame (it had been said that cities far away could be glimpsed in it like mirages, and that should an enemy ship appear, the rays of the sun could be reflected on it with enough intensity to envelop it in flames). Silt obliterated and widened the mole, and all that was left of the island of Pharos was the quarter where Mohammed Ali was to build his favourite palace, Ras-el-Tin (Cape of Figs), commanding the entrance to the harbour.

Modern Alexandria is a planned city much of it built with gains from the cotton trade. At the west end of the sweeping semi-circular corniche facing the sea is Ras-el-Tin and at the east end, Montazah Palace. Inland the city has many sporting clubs, theatres, cinemas, tea rooms, restaurants, hotels and as has been mentioned, a shopping centre where you will find the most reasonable prices in the Mediterranean.

Montazah Palace could not be on a more ideal site. It is built on a knoll and its long driveway passes up through an eucalyptus forest to the front entrance. Three sides of the palace are surrounded by one of the most beautiful parks in Egypt and the fourth side faces the Mediterranean. From a distance out at sea it must look like a pale pink icing palace straight out of a fairy book, with frosted towers and crenellated edgings.

This ex royal palace has a casino on the ground floor and the other floors have been opened as a museum where you can visit the royal apartments. These retain some of the furniture used by the late King Farouk and his family.

The great verandahs and balconies are colourfully tiled and there are endearing statues in white marble of sleeping lions placed here and there in the park and at the entrance to the palace.

Practically next door to the palace and in the same park is the air-conditioned Palestine Hotel built in 1964 to accommodate Arab kings and heads of state attending a conference. On the ground floor there is a lounge, bar, cafeteria and a dining room which can seat 180 people; also a nightclub. The outdoor terrace overlooks the sea. Montazah Bay is fringed with beach cabins which can be rented for short periods or for the season. Guests can join in all sorts of activities, swimming, sailing, beach games, fishing, waterskiing, and there are motor boats for hire.

Sightseeing is not difficult as Alexandria is laid out on the grid system used in many modern cities. A number 8 bus can take you to Ras-el-Tin Palace, now used for government purposes and official entertainment. Its apartments are sumptuous especially the Chandelier Room, remarkable for the spectacular crystal and gilt chandelier. It is reflected in a magnificent round green marble table and casts shimmering light on a parquet floor inlaid with mother of pearl.

It was in the Attendants' Hall with its red plush chairs, on 25 July 1952, that King Farouk sat with the American Ambassador waiting for the last paper he was to sign in Egypt. The instrument of abdication was executed on the green marble table in the next room, now called the Salle d'Abdication.

As the palace has ceased to be a museum it may not be possible to visit it. However there are other fascinating places and most are within a short distance of the centre of town.

Excavations in the '60s at Kom el Dekka, near the Roman Museum disclosed a Graeco-Roman open air theatre, the only one of its kind in Egypt built probably towards the end of the second century. It was discovered after levelling an artificial hill and dismantling an old Napoleonic fort. Excitement was intense as the archaeologists went deeper and gradually uncovered the ancient building.

There are two entrances to the site, one from Abdel Moneim Street close to the railway station and the other from

Saphia Zaghloul Street. You walk along banks set with flower beds and edged with trees to gaze down at the stage and imagine it peopled with actors and actresses of long ago. Thirteen rows of white marble seating radiate upward from it in a semi-circle. Gone are the niches at the top which at one time were supported by black, white, grey and green pillars. Capitols from broken columns still show some of the original ornamentation.

Other antiquities in Alexandria which merit explanation are Pompey's Pillar and the Serapeum which is thought to lie beneath it. Being of Greek origin the Ptolemies encouraged Greeks to settle in Alexandria and it became the intellectual capital of the Hellenic world, the very fountain head of learning. Its advanced ideas in scientific studies and the establishment of its enormous library attracted scholars from all around the Mediterranean.

The founder of the Ptolemaic dynasty (304-330 B.C.) Ptolemy 1 thought that the best way to forge Egyptian-Greek relationship was through a divinity acceptable to both. The conception of Osiris, whose reincarnation on earth was the bull Apis, was extended to include Plato, the Greek god of healing and other gods. The various attributes of these were crystallised in Seraphis for whom a beautiful temple, the Serapeum, was built in the city. It was erected on a plateau dominating Alexandria and was reached by a hundred steps. Porticoes lined the facade and, within the sacred courts, a shrine contained a statue of Seraphis wrought, it was said, of silver, gold, copper, lead and tin. It sparkled with emeralds, sapphires and topazes. When the temple was destroyed the statue vanished. A larger more magnificent temple was built by Hadrian and new statues were presented. Fortunately one of these statues has survived to this day; the sacred bull Apis with a sun disc between the horns. It can be seen at the Graeco-Roman museum. The temple itself no longer exists.

Pompey's Pillar was erected by Pompey, a Roman prefect in A.D. 302 to the Emperor Diocletian. The shaft is of polished red granite, topped by a Corinthian capital. It was raised to Diocletian because he gave food to the people during a frightful famine. The pillar stands on an open space on the highest spot in the city so that it appears much higher than its 99 feet. It tapers from 9 feet at its base to 8 feet at its summit. A sphinx crouches by its side. Fragments of stone and columns which lie around the base may have belonged to the Serapeum.

Close by Pompey's Pillar you come to the catacombs. They were discovered by accident in 1900 when a donkey and cart vanished from view down a yawning hole that suddenly opened. You can go down three levels by a spiral staircase, and visit various funerary chambers. There is a mixture of Roman-Greek and Egyptian decoration the latter in the form of the wings of Horus – and there are statues of a woman and a man in Pharaonic costume. You will be taken to the private funerary chamber of Emperor Caracalla who was inordinately fond of horses. Certainly there is a collection of bones, supposedly from his favourite steeds, in a large cabinet.

Christianity in Egypt spread from Alexandria where St. Mark first preached the gospel. He was subsequently martyred there. His mission spread so widely that it encompassed North East Africa from the Mediterranean to Abyssinia. The Copts have a long history of devotion. Their calendar begins from the 'Era of the Martyrs' when they suffered great persecution under Diocletian and chose death rather than deny their faith. Many fled to the Sinai and Libyan deserts to continue their devotion in caves and ancient temples thus sowing the seeds of monastic life. Later St. Anthony withdrew to a deserted fort on the east bank of the Nile opposite the Fayoum. During the next twenty years he lived alone but word of his piety spread to such an extent that he re-emerged and was responsible for founding the Coptic monasticism which became the model for that of other forms of Christianity. In 1897 E. L. Butcher in his book *The Story of the Church of Egypt,* published in London, wrote: 'The extent to which the population became monks and nuns could hardly be believed if it were not attested by contemporary writers, who travelled to Egypt to see this strange thing for themselves.'

The Coptic Patriarch is always chosen from among the monks of the Convent of St. Anthony in the eastern desert of Egypt, near the Red Sea. A Coptic priest may or may not be married under certain complex conditions and these are best explained by Edward Lane in his famous book *The Modern Egyptians* written in Egypt during the years 1833-35.

A priest must have been a deacon; he must be without bodily defect, at least thirty three years of age and a person who has either never married, or has married but one wife, a virgin, before he became a priest for he cannot marry after. If a priest's wife dies he cannot marry again; nor may the widow of a priest marry a second husband. A priest may be of the order of monks; and consequently unmarried.

In the Graeco-Roman Museum you can see a collection of 5th century stucco paintings of saints and coloured geometrical designs which come from monasteries to the west of Alexandria. Also textiles woven from wool and flax with animal and plant designs. Others have scenes from Greek mythology. In the same hall there is an alabaster statue representing the Good Shepherd with a lamb held across the shoulders and two smaller lambs sitting on either side of His feet.

This museum has a maze of bright rooms housing exhibits from different periods of the city's history. The beautifully preserved statue of the Aphis bull excavated from ruins near Pompey's Pillar, imposing figures of gods and Roman rulers, fine golden jewellery and an incredible collection of coins. Only a few of the latter are on exhibition but the museum possesses some 50,000. Most fascinating of all perhaps is a beautiful collection of Tanagras. These tiny terra cotta figurines are of inestimable value and still retain some of their original colouring, blue, green and pink. From rounded shoulders their becoming robes, of the time of Cleopatra, fall in graceful folds to their tiny feet. Each stauette stands in a different posture and they are very well displayed on glass shelving.

A passage leads to a garden and once again you are

conscious of the continual dry, sunny Egyptian weather, for, on display in the gardens, are further finds – as safe out of doors as under cover. One comprises two large tombs of the first and third centuries. There is a statue of Ramses 11 with his daughter, a bust of Anthony as Osiris and two granite sphinxes from Heliopolis. The garden is delightfully quiet, save for the chirping of many birds, and if you have time to sit for a while no one will disturb you.

Alexandria's winding corniche with its string of white hotels is treeless so the focal point is the Midan Saad Zaghloul with its wide avenues edged with palm trees and flower beds. A statue of the famous Egyptian statesman, Saad Zaghloul, is surrounded by green lawns and flower troughs. Benches are placed conveniently close to the corniche so that strollers can sit and enjoy a view of the shimmering turquoise sea a few yards away.

Zaghloul is posed in a standing position and, like so many statues of Ramses 11, one foot is placed forward as if the statesman could not resist walking straight into the cool waves of the Mediterranean. A jauntily placed fez protects his head from the sun.

From these gardens there is a lovely view over the whole bay which curls in a semicircle for about ten kilometres. To the north, where the famous Pharos once stood, is Fort Kait Bey on the very tip of the harbour. This medieval structure looks like a Ruritanian Beau Geste fort with its turrets, loopholes and crenellated battlements. It is now a naval museum. On the first floor there are paintings and dioramas of Pharaonic boats and sea battles. Succeeding halls and floors have other paintings, dioramas and models of Egyptian boats and scenes of naval history up to the present day.

Everyone who has heard of modern Alexandria knows about its famous beaches. The best perhaps are those at Stanley, Glymenopoulo and Sidi-Bishr – not to mention Montazah and Ma'mura. 'One of the most fashionable without doubt is Al Agami to the west, which is referred to as the Saint Tropez of Egypt. You can hire boats, go fishing, play volley ball, swim or just laze.

4 The Mediterranean Coast and Oases

Less than 100 miles to the west of Alexandria lies Alamein. The name seems prophetic for in Arabic it means 'Two Flags'. Over thirty years ago the vigorous youth of two armies was locked in combat here. Today thousands of them lie enshrined beneath their flags. Alamein is now a place of pilgrimage.

A visit to the cemeteries from Alexandria within the day needs an early start. Once beyond the outskirts of the city you drive along a shimmering asphalt road which stretches, a thin black line, between extensive fig groves, which in turn give way to desert, and are tended by Beduin. Just when you think you have come to the end of cultivation another grove comes into view. These plantations end abruptly. The lonely railway line to Mersa Matruh is on the left and the scrub covered desert stretches as far as the eye can see.

To the right the fawn sand gradually merges into startingly white dunes and beyond them you suddenly see the Mediterranean. In bright sunlight the sea is an unbelievable delphinium blue. I have never seen the Mediterranean in the South of France or in Italy the same irridescent blue as along this coastal landscape. It is luminous yet 'blurred' – as the bloom coats a Malaga grape. The whiteness of the sand dunes and exotic blue of the sea continue mile after mile, and have such an hypnotic effect that time does not seem to matter.

As you draw closer to Alamein the road gradually rises and at the same time the sand dunes flatten so that you get a better view of the sea. If it is early summer specks of yellow and green by the roadside grow into laburnum trees, heavy with blossom, close by the Alamein Rest House. The last time I was there an Egyptian army encampment stretched along both sides of the roadway. Spiky cactus plants edge a little roadway off to the desert on the left side to a gateway which leads to an arched white cloister. A plaque reads:

> Within this cloister are inscribed the names of soldiers and airmen of the British Commonwealth and Empire who died fighting on land or in the air where two continents meet, and to whom the fortunes of war devised a known and honoured grave with their fellows who rest in this cemetery with their comrades in arms of the Royal Navy. They preserved for the West the link with the East and turned the tide of war.

Through the central arch you can see an unadorned high cross and between plots of green grass there are neat beds of sweet smelling roses. It might be England. Flowers grow among the simple white gravestones. Everything is quiet, the individual graves beautifully kept. Badges of the various regiments are carved on the top of the tombstones. Four are linked together which have no names but have the words: 'Four soldiers of the 1939-1945 war – Known unto God'.

The tombstones look alike but the engravings are as individual as the men who rest beneath the sand. I wrote a few down at random. Private C. R. Honey:

'Deep in our heart a memory is kept
And we who loved him will never forget.'

Gunner J. White R.A. aged 25:

'No loved one stood around him to bid a fond farewell.'

Lieutenant A. G. Bagshawe R.A. aged 22:

'He maketh me to lie down in green pastures. He leadeth me beside still waters'.

Corporal C. Callender R.C.N. aged 28:

'He gave his life in the hope of a better world.'

As you return to the cloisters there is another plaque which reads:

'1939-1945. The land on which this cemetery stands is the

11. *A Nile passenger steamer*
12. *Irrigation by water wheel at Dendera on the Nile*

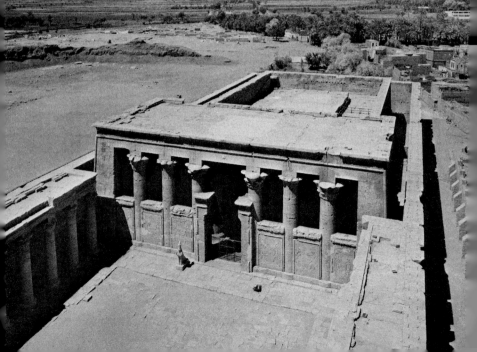

gift of the Egyptian people for the perpetual resting place of the sailors, soldiers and airmen who are honoured here.'

The German cemetery is a few miles further on. The German memorial is designed as a large tower, somewhat like a mediaeval castle. It is also open to the sky and within its precincts are large alcoves, each with a mass grave. Beneath a massive sarcophagus in every one lie five hundred soldiers of the renowned Afrika Korps. The arch over each bears the names of the men, some from Munich, from Dresden from Hamburg and other parts of Germany. The Rommel memorial is in a white enclosure.

Along the road further to the west there is the Italian cemetery with a small white museum at the entrance containing charts, maps and weapons which were used during the second world war. The Italian memorial itself is in the form of a high cone with a vaulted ceiling. Half the wall is glass, the rest is inscribed with the names of the fallen. An altar with a statue of the Virgin Mary is usually covered with flowers. A staircase winds upwards to the ceiling, which has oblong openings. The wind comes in through them with a sighing sound. It is a sad but beautiful place.

Because Alamein is the narrowest point between the Qattara depression to the south (a curious vast basin of sand and salt marshes edged by sheer cliffs) and the sea, it was chosen as the best place by the allies to give battle to the Axis forces and exclude them from the delta. Today it is calm and peaceful and its blue waters across white sand inviting for those who enjoy swimming. Only the quiet well kept cemeteries are a reminder of the pitiless conflict which once raged here.

A bare half hour's drive along the coast from Alamein will bring you to a small exclusive seaside resort, Sidi Abdul Rahman. The Hotel Alamein has 40 double rooms and there are 10 villas each with four double rooms. They are completely self contained down to a barbecue and a sunshade at the water's edge. Each villa has a servant and garage and its own private beach. Linen is changed daily and meals can be

13. *The Colossi of Memnon at Thebes*
14. *The open court at Edfu temple as seen from the Pylon*

had at the hotel or cooked in the villa. There is no noise, only the lapping of the waves. With congenial friends it is a perfect place to get away from it all for a few days.

Further along the coast at R'As El Hekma a 20,000-acre site has been designated as a National Reserve in perpetuity to contain a new resort planned to be of the highest international standards for the discerning holiday maker. Architects will wed Moslem and Coptic architecture with modern amenities. The key hotel is to be on the highest point of the peninsula, overlooking the sea where Cleopatra once had her summer palace, a site now occupied by the late King Farouk's summer residence. From this vantage point there are panoramic views along the coastline. The central village will be located on the eastern side of the peninsula on hilly terrain overlooking gardens, a golf course and sandy coves. There will be eucalyptus and fig groves and a land-locked marina with a narrow outlet to the sea. The 'Fishing Village', different in character from the greener part on the eastern side, will cluster around the harbour. Apartments and self contained units, furnished and completely equipped, will be offered for sale or rent. The existing settlement at the railway station is to be extended to house those involved with servicing the new resort.

Mersa Matruh lies about 200 kilometres west of Alexandria and again brings back memories of the last war. In the headland across the harbour is 'Rommel's Grotto' – an underground headquarters cut into the rock and reinforced. Today the town is a most enticing place the sandy beach being whiter, if that were possible, than that at Alamein. The approach to it from Alamein is along the straight desert road which, during the heat of the day, shimmers in the vivid sunlight. On the outskirts the roadway climbs gradually and suddenly over the brow of a hill Mersa Matruh, like a colourful oasis, comes into sight. It edges a large emerald and sapphire lagoon with white stretches of beach and is cut off from the Mediterranean by a chain of huge rocks. Cleopatra felt its glamour and an isolated rock out to sea is known as 'Cleopatra's rock'. It was here that she had a pavilion where she stayed with Mark Antony before the battle of Actium (31 B.C.) following which Egypt fell under the Roman yoke.

The waters of the lake west of the present port cover the site of the dockyards which were used by the Egyptian fleet under the Ptolemies. On the eastern extremity of this lake you can still see the ruins of a stone quay.

The little town boasts a set of traffic lights which have been known to show red and green simultaneously but traffic is not heavy and the camels and donkeys take no notice. The colourful robes of the Beduin women mingle with the black ones of the townsfolk. Many of the local people are North African emigrants or Greeks, others belong to an Arab tribe called Awled Ali, the Sons of Ali. From wayside cafes visiting Beduin sip coffee in white robes or burnooses, watching town life go by. Small shops are full of foreign consumer goods and many of things are cheaper than in the larger cities. Sunset is the favourite shopping time. Many unusual things are to be found by visitors; necklaces of mother of pearl, glass beads, slippers of gazelle skin and rugs made of a mixture of sheep and camel wool.

On the hills, around the lakes there are remains of an ancient church and many grottoes. The port is a prosperous one and has served at various times as a naval base. It is close to the railway line running along the coast from Alexandria to Sollum, which is almost on the Libyan frontier. The road from Mersa Matruh to Sollum leaves the coast and continues to Sidi Barrani some 420 kilometres away.

Another route leading from Mersa Matruh, but this time not by rail or the usual conventional road, is inland to the Oasis of Siwa – along a telegraph line! The way is straightforward and nearly a hundred miles of the 190 are asphalted. The telegraph poles mark the whole route but nevertheless if you go even slightly off course and lose sight of a pole you can easily go in the wrong direction and get lost. The journey should never be undertaken with less than two vehicles in convoy.

It must be remembered that none of the oases are geared for tourism at the time this book goes to print and before making plans to visit such places it is necessary to consult the Egyptian Tourist Administration.

5 Food and Drink

The Egyptians love good food and have many special dishes. Unlike people who prefer to keep their recipes secret, they are always keen to share the intricacies of their delicious cooking with visitors. Hospitality insists that a full table must be kept at all times in case of unexpected guests. On the face of it there must be great waste but in fact this is not so. Custom demands that the guest should have a lavish choice of dishes but later on members of the family, then the servants and, in the desert, even casual strangers consume what is left. The present groaning table stems from this.

You are invariably pressed to eat more food than you possibly can. It is quite polite to refuse. The host must insist because it is traditional. A favourite Arabic proverb is that 'The amount of food eaten shows the regard in which the guest holds the host'. Perhaps the best illustration of this is the story of a well-known diplomat who was invited to an outdoor feast near the Pyramids of Giza. He had an invalid's stomach and a small appetite. He knew it would be difficult to convince his host of this. He thought he had solved the problem by accepting the invitation but, to avoid hurting his host by eating too little, requested that there should be only one course. Without betraying Egyptian hospitality and at the same time bowing to his guest's request, a single course was produced of an enormous whole barbecued lamb. When it was carved it was seen to be full of chickens, the chickens in turn contained quail and these were stuffed with smaller birds!

To the townsfolk and Beduin alike hospitality is traditional. In the desert the stranger is the 'guest of Allah' – even a potential enemy who requires shelter and food cannot be refused and once he has eaten his host's bread and salt, he may claim sanctuary. Eating together is almost a sacred rite. To pick out a particularly delicious morsel from your plate and profer it to a friend is considered polite and must not be refused.

To be a guest at a desert feast is a delightful and unusual experience but not unfortunately given to many tourists as the visitor must usually know some local dignitary before he is invited. However caravan tents can be erected by arrangement for tourist parties if desired. Morsi Gabry of Karnak Bazaar behind Shepheard's Hotel will arrange one near the Pyramids, complete with oriental band and belly dancer – not to mention Arab horse dancing which is particularly effective to watch by moonlight after a satisfying meal.

Such desert feasts take a long time to prepare and there are usually a large number of guests. The 'piece de resistance' is invariably a whole sheep roasted over a barbecue pit until the meat is thoroughly cooked and crispy outside. The guests sit cross legged on thick hand woven carpets or cushions at low tables. First the roast mutton is displayed on a great platter for all to see and admire and other large dishes are produced some with mounds of saffron coloured rice covered with pine kernels. Sometimes forks and knives are used, sometimes not. If not it is quite easy to eat with the fingers dipping pieces of bread into the various dishes, putting pieces of meat in your mouth and then making small balls of the rice and doing likewise. Only the right hand should be used. Finger bowls will be produced to dip your fingers in later. The meat course will be followed by sweet dishes and fruit.

The coffee or tea which finishes the feast is poured with much ceremony. Sometimes a coffee pot may be two or three feet tall yet the coffee pourer (who is not chosen but offers his services as he has mastered the art and enjoys it) has to hold the pot a good foot or two up in the air from the tiny cup or glass and pour it, like a barman a cocktail, without spilling a drop. After you drink the first cup it is filled again with the same elan. You may refuse the third cup. Should the beverage be tea, the first cup will be sweet, the second sweeter and the third sweetest of all. Should the drink be coffee it is often served with cardamom seeds which give it a spicy flavour.

Whether a feast is held in a large tent or under palm trees it is customary to remove your shoes before walking to your place over carpeting.

All restaurants and cafes can produce European food but, if you order familiar things, it is as well to remember that beef can be tough, veal is scarce and pork is not popular in a Moslem country although in the luxury and first class hotels frozen meats are imported. The best local meat by far is lamb. Chicken and fish are also a good choice. Vegetables and fruit are always fresh and of good quality.

The excellent lamb and mutton raised in the Middle East is the favourite meat of the people. It is plentiful and not as expensive as beef and there are numerous ways of cooking and serving it. 'Kebab' is particularly suited to Western taste and you might like to try one of the recipes at home such as this one:

LAMB KEBAB
Yield – 6 Kebabs on skewers
Cooking Time – about 15 minutes

Ingredients
6 Tomatoes
6 Onions (small)
$1\frac{1}{2}$ lb Lamb Shoulder
$\frac{1}{2}$ cup French dressing – made according to taste
$\frac{1}{2}$ clove of garlic

Method
Cut lamb into one inch cubes. Pour French dressing over the lamb – and add a split clove of garlic or onion juice if desired. Let stand at least one hour, or overnight in the refrigerator. Alternate lamb, tomatoes and onions on metal skewers. Allow space between for thorough cooking. Season with salt and pepper. Grill some 3 inches from source of heat (charcoal gives a delicious flavour) for about 15 minutes. Turn

to brown evenly. You can also add mushrooms and bacon on the skewers if you wish.

Kuftas are often served with kebab and are threaded on the skewers at the same time. They are far more delicious than sausages and easy to make. Minced lamb is flavoured with pine kernels, chopped parsley and seasoning and then formed into sausages. They can be served in the same way as kebab and, as much of Egyptian cooking is done by rule of thumb, I thought I would not bother about quantities but watch an hotel chef and learn that way.

My chef cut some choice slices off a leg of lamb and put them through a mincer over a scrubbed board. He beat the mixture with a rolling pin, placed it in a stone mortar and beat it again with a pestle adding salt, pepper, lemon juice and parlsey now and then. He moulded bits of the mixture into sausage shapes and pushed them onto metal skewers separated with small onions and tomatoes. He then placed the skewers over a charcoal grill and cooked them slowly, turning the skewers now and then so that they browned evenly all round.

Fresh young vine leaves are used to make *Mahshi*. The leaves are softened and blanched (they can also be bought in tins) and a mixture of chopped or minced meat is mixed with flavoured rice and rolled in them. They can be cooked in various ways one being to place them over water on a layer of bones in a saucepan covered with sliced tomatoes and whole garlic and simmer until tender. Mahshi can also be encased in cabbage leaves or young marrows instead of vine leaves. Most delicious of all perhaps is *Shikh el Mahshi*, a mixture of meat, onion and parsley, fried first and then stuffed into small aubergines baked in tomato sauce until golden brown and served hot with rice.

Pigeon is a dish every Egyptian loves. It is usually split down the middle and grilled over charcoal and literally melts in the mouth.

Mezza is a sort of hors d'oeuvre with which most meals begin. It is also somewhat like the Swedish *smorgasbord* or the Danish *smoerbrod* in that it consists of salads, sauces, small pieces of meat, fish and other titbits in several little dishes. One of the most delicious is Tahena sauce, an aromatic blend of sesame seeds and oil with a hint of garlic whipped to the creamy consistency of mayonnaise. Two other sauces or 'dips' to use with Mezza are Babaghanoug and Cucumber yoghourt salad. Here is how they are made:

BABAGHANOUG
Bake two small eggplants in the oven. Cool and peel and place in colander to drain. Mash or grind the eggplant. Add $\frac{3}{4}$ tablespoons tahina, $\frac{3}{4}$ crushed cloves of garlic and 1 cup yoghourt. Mix well and then add the juice of 1 lemon. Chill.

CUCUMBER YOGHOURT
Place 1 cup (carton) of yoghourt in a bowl that has been rubbed with garlic. Peel and slice 1 or 2 cucumbers into the yoghourt. Sprinkle with dried mint and mix. Chill.

My husband likens the Egyptian *Ta'amia* to the British fish and chips. It is inexpensive to make and can be eaten alone or with mezza. There are many recipes. Here is one:

TA'AMIA
1 cup dried and crushed haricot beans
Parsley
Green coriander
Onion   A sprinkling of each
Garlic
Salt
1 teaspoon bicarbonate of soda
1 handful bread soaked in water
Wash the beans and soak them overnight. Put all the ingredients through the mincing machine and mix them well. To soften the dough pound it a little in the mortar. Mix in the bicarbonate of soda. Leave the mixture to rest for an hour of two. Make mixture into small round balls and deep fry in oil.

Arabic bread is served with every meal and is most useful with mezza when there are so many sauces to 'dip'. All housewives who make their own bread keep a 'starter'. This is a small ball of dough from the previous baking. It is left in salty water overnight and wheat flour is added to it and then worked into a smooth stretchy mass. This in turn is kneaded into a roll from which 'rounds' are cut for the bread. The dough has no milk or shortening. A loaf is flat and round, about 10 inches in diameter. It rises in the oven, but sinks as it cools. The villagers like their bread for its chewy texture and everyone loves it for sandwiches. It can easily be torn in two and stuffed with cheese, meat or vegetables to become sandwiches. Visitors are a little apprehensive about taking a whole loaf, but it is empty so it is not as filling as it looks. If you want a picnic you can go into any cafe and order meat or cheese to put in Arabic bread and there is no need for forks or knives – or indeed plates. In hotels it is often torn in two and then crisped in the oven to make Melba toast.

Egyptians are very fond of fish. In Pharaonic times they enjoyed mullet, carp, perch, tigerfish and eel. They knew how to dry and salt fish and even had an early version of tartare sauce made from the juice of sour grapes. Many people claim that Mediterranean fish is not as tasty as that from colder waters but it depends how quickly it is cooked. Nothing can be nicer than trout caught and grilled immediately in a little butter. It tastes even better if you have just caught it yourself! Luckily there are several fish restaurants and it is difficult to say where giant prawns en broche taste the best. There are the Seahorse and Good Shot on the outskirts of Maadi overlooking the Nile not far from Cairo and there is the famous Casino Zephyrion at Abou Kir not far from Alexandria. The latter is owned by Periclis Tsaparis. He is not only always there in person to greet guests but helps to serve, take down orders, and seems to be everywhere at once when the restaurant is busy – which is always! Every kind of fish is displayed for your inspection in large open deep freeze cabinets where you can choose what you wish to eat. The shrimps or prawns are so large they look like langoustes. Coated with butter and seasoned they are served en broche and taste crispy and milky at the same time. Perhaps the best accolade I can give the Casino Zephyrion is that three gourmets hired a car in Cairo and went all the way to Abou Kir for luncheon reckoning that their fish meal was more than worth the time and money spent.

Egyptian sweets are not for those who wish to lose weight or are on a diet but when away on holiday such thoughts are pushed aside. Perhaps the best known is *Baclawa* which is cooked through the Middle East and there are many methods of making it. It is made of many layers of paper thin dough with a filling of crushed nuts and sugar between them. Honey is poured over the pastry when it comes hot from the oven to give it a translucency and a rich flavour. The pastry takes a long time to make at home because it must be rolled very thin. Squares of *baclawa* are sold in shops from large trays. They may be eaten there or taken home.

Most hotel menus have *Baclawa* and its twin *Konafa* and the latter is also made in different ways. Here is the easiest method:

KONAFA
6 shredded wheat biscuits (breakfast cereal may be used)
1 cup chopped toasted almonds
1 cup light corn syrup
$\frac{1}{4}$ cup (packed) light brown sugar
$\frac{1}{4}$ cup granulated sugar
$\frac{1}{2}$ cup water
2 tablespoons butter
1 cup whipped cream.

Place the shredded wheat biscuits on a baking sheet well greased with butter. Heat biscuits in a moderate oven (350°) for about 10 minutes. Crumble 3 of the biscuits into a 9-inch pie pan which has been well greased with butter. Sprinkle the almonds over this layer. Crumble the remaining three biscuits over the almonds. Combine the corn syrup, sugars, water and butter in a one quart saucepan. Heat until sugars and butter are melted and the mixture is well blended. Pour over the shredded wheat and almonds. Let stand at room temperature until all the mixture is absorbed (about 2 to 3 hours). Cut into

wedges and serve with a generous spoonful of whipped cream.
About 12 servings.

As sweets or desserts are often a headache for hostesses I
thought I would give four more tempting ones:

BASSBUSA

3 cups sugar	Syrup:
2 cups yoghourt	1½ cups sugar
2 cups semolina (cream of wheat)	1½ cups water
1 tbls baking soda	Boil 5 min and add few
	drops lemon juice.

Mix the sugar, yoghourt, semolina and soda together and
place in baking dish in 350°F oven. Bake until bright brown
and then remove, pour the prepared syrup over it, slice and
return to oven until baked.

ESHES SERAYA or PALACE BREAD

Heat ½ lb honey with ¼ lb butter until the mixture thickens.
Add 4 ozs white breadcrumbs. Cook all together in a
saucepan, stirring until it has become a homogeneous mass.
Turn out on to plate and when cold it will be like a soft cake
and can be cut into triangular portions. This sweet is always
served with a cream which is skimmed off the top of quantities
of milk cooked very slowly until a thick skin forms on top, so
stiff that when separated from the milk it can be rolled up. A
little of this cream is placed on top of each portion of the
Palace Bread.

UM ALI or ALI'S MOTHER'S PASTRY

2¼ cups flour	½ cup raisins or nuts
6 cups milk	1 egg
2 cups sugar	¼ tsp. salt
1 cup cream	½ cup water plus 1 tbls butter for frying

Mix flour, salt and egg together. Add water to make soft
dough. Divide dough into 20 pieces. Cover with towel for
about 15-30 minutes. Now roll each piece with a roller to the
thickness of a coin. Fry it light brown in butter. Crumble 10

into a greased baking dish, add the raisins and then crumble the remaining 10 over the raisins. Press down well with your hand. Put the sugar into the boiling milk and stir until dissolved then pour it over the pan. Then pour the cream over it. Bake about 30 minutes in medium oven. Serve hot.

BALAH EL SHAM

1 teacup water	4 eggs
1 teacup flour	1 teacup oil for frying
$\frac{1}{4}$ teacup butter	

Heat butter in pan, add the water and let it boil. Then add the flour gradually, stirring the mixture quickly until it forms a dough. Take off from heat and cool. Add one egg at a time. Cut in forms and fry in boiling oil on slow heat. When fried dip in syrup. Or after adding eggs make into balls $1\frac{1}{2}''$, stuff with cheese etc. Bake in 350°F oven until brown (8/10 minutes).

Despite the cry that coffee is the main drink of those in the Middle East is does not always apply. In Egypt tea is equally important and particularly loved by the fallaheen. Both tea and coffee are sweeter than in Europe. If you do not take sugar at all just say so. If you like a little ask for *Mazbout*. Coffee making is a great art and, even in a tiny shop in a village, great care is taken to give the guest coffee just as he would wish it – and always piping hot. You can order 'French Coffee', which is served in a large cup, or 'Turkish Coffee' which is much stronger and is served in a small one. The latter is very black and as heartening as a cocktail.

Turkish coffee purists insist that the beans be roasted over a charcoal fire and ground with a stone pestle and mortar. One heaped teaspoonful of ground coffee and one of sugar is used per serving and it is made in a tiny coffee jug holding two fluid ounces. The water and sugar are boiled together in this little brass or silver pot, then the coffee is added and stirred well. When it foams to the top it is quickly removed from the flame and the liquid subsides. The pot is put on the flame again and the same thing happens. It should do this three times. Then the coffee is ready to be served. Sometimes cardamom seeds are added. Your coffee can be poured from a tiny individual pot. If you are one of many guests it is often made in a large coffee pot which a safragi will carry with a group of little cups without handles stacked one inside the other in his hand. He fills each top cup in turn and offers it to the guests. If there are a number of guests the oldest is given the first cup. This can be a little awkward!

Merchants will offer you coffee in their shops. Indeed wherever you go you are offered coffee, although this sometimes changes to a fruit drink or coca cola. You are brought your drink by a safragi and drink it alone, as your host is not expected to join you. If he did he would be drinking all day. At one time it was considered a discourtesy to refuse but, again as you yourself may be visiting several places, it is perfectly in order to refuse a drink if you do not want one.

Coffee is served piping hot and the grounds will have sunk to the bottom, so it is never stirred (you are not given a spoon, so you will not be tempted to do this) and you will find as soon as the thinner liquid on the top is drunk the grounds may get in your mouth if you persist in trying to finish it. From a full cup of coffee you drink half. Arabic coffee pots (small or large) can be bought and coffee made like the above at home. Sugar is added according to taste.

Local fruit drinks are most refreshing. Just plain orange or grapefruit juice iced is delicious but there are several mixtures. One is called *Khoshaf*. It is flavoured with rosewater and grenadine and at the bottom of your glass you will find raisins, apricots, peeled almonds and pine kernels. Another is *Doom* (pronounced 'dome') a drink made in Upper Egypt during the spring when the doom trees bear fruit. This fan leaved tree from tropical Africa grows well in Aswan and Luxor and often reaches a height of 50 feet. Its wood is very hard and has economic value. A glass of Doom should especially appeal to Americans and Canadians as it has a distinctive maple syrup flavour and is served iced.

As early as Pharaonic times the Egyptians made beer from baked barley dough fermented in date sweetened water. To quote Athenaeus, an Egyptian who lived during the third century A.D. 'Those who drank this beer were so pleased with it that they sang and danced.' On the other hand surviving papyri warn: 'Do not get drunk in the places in which they drink beer, for fear that people repeat words which may have gone out of thy mouth, without having perception of having uttered them!'

Whatever effect the praises and warnings of the past 'Stella' beer is enjoyed by visitors today and, as its name implies, it is very like Belgian 'Stella Artois'. There is nothing like this cooling drink to revive one after a day's sightseeing. It is very good and served ice cold – but one word of warning. Stella only comes in larger bottles; perfect if you are really thirsty or if there are two of you but it can be a little heady.

The art of wine making in Egypt dates back as far as records exist. In ancient times the vine was imported from Asia and wine was ascribed to the gods. In Greece to Dionysus, in Egypt to Osiris and there were special funerary wines. Certainly vineyards were carefully cultivated as far back as 3200 B.C. and, then as now, they were heavily taxed. Tomb paintings sometimes have backgrounds of vine trellises. In the tomb of Sennufer the ceiling is sculptured with hanging bunches of grapes. Wine was aged in amphorae and sealed with plaster stoppers often bearing the name of the grower, the year and the name of the vineyard. Stacks of these and other wine jars have been found in tombs.

The finest wines come from parts of the delta and the oases. The best was known as 'Mareotic'. According to Athenaeus this was 'white and sweet and good for the breath and digestible'. For centuries this wine was highly regarded not only in Egypt but especially in Rome. During the seventh century the Arabs swept through Egypt and as their religion forebade wine, viticulture gradually declined. However grapes continued to be grown for the table both in the area beyond Alexandria and in the Fayoum. The grape known as 'Fayoumi' has always been a favourite in the market and it is the first to ripen each season. The berries are medium sized but the flavour is excellent and the fruit very juicy.

In recent years an increasing demand for wine, both in Egypt and abroad, has brought viticulture back on a commercial scale and the area chosen is the same as that which produced the famous Mareotic wine of long ago. Near Lake Mareotis, some ninety kilometres from Alexandria, the calceous soil is perfect for vines. The venture was begun during the last century by a Greek named Gianaclis and the present day vast vineyards still bear his name.

I was taken with my husband and some friends to visit them on a sunny spring day at the end of April. We drove some 70 kilometres along the desert road from Alexandria towards Cairo and then turned abruptly north to Gianaclis along a narrow metalled road. The name desert road still remains although in recent years, through irrigation, much of the land on either side is cultivated and when we turned north we passed between lines of casuarinas and reaforestation areas. After some 15 kilometres of the Gianaclis Road we came to a village of the same name which is the beginning of the wine area. It was a surprise to learn that the vineyards stretch over twenty thousand acres including five villages for the workers.

The village was a most pleasant little place with its own mosque, school, club, cafeteria, dispensary and so on. We halted at a rest house for a refreshing drink; not wine – that was to come later. We spent a fascinating day being taken over the vineyards, the winery and watching the people at work.

It is interesting that the vines grow on the flat, sandy desert soil instead of the more usual terraces of Europe and that they are watered only about five times during the growing season by the simple process of flooding the vineyard. Each section is protected from the desert winds by strategically planted wind breaks of pine trees which produce a sighing sound in the breeze. Later we tasted some of the wines at a special little marble bar with a marble sink where, after a sip, glasses were thoroughly washed before trying another brand. I asked if there were good and bad vintage years and received the surprising if logical reply that, as the climatic conditions were predictable, the vintages are consistent and show little variation.

15. *The statue of Horus at Edfu*
16. *The statue of Tutankhamen at Karnak*

Wine is a difficult subject to write about when you are like me not an expert so I am only able to tell the reader what is available so that he may suit his own taste. Personally I prefer white wine to red and dry to sweet. My favourite white wine was the second driest 'Village'. The range from the driest to the sweetest white wine is as follows:

Clos Matamir
Gianaclis Village
Cru des Ptolemees
Nefertiti
Reine Cleopatre

'Cru des Ptolemees' is a very nice dry white wine and is usually available. The two sweet white wines 'Nefertiti' and 'Reine Cleopatre' are also readily available in most hotels and restaurants. Of the reds 'Omar Khayyam' is the most popular and tastes like a full bodied chianti. I found 'Pharaons' more to my taste. 'Kokkineli' and 'Vin de Messe' are sweeter.

Rosé wines are made either by leaving the black grape skins in the fermenting vats for a suitable time or by blending a white wine with a smaller proportion of red. Of these 'Rubis d'Egypte' and 'Petzina' are very good. 'Muscat d'Egypte' can be drunk like a sherry or a madeira. There are many more wines and the visitor will enjoy tasting and making his own choice.

Gianaclis also make brandy, port, zibib and rum – the latter from pure cane sugar not molasses. The distilleries are in Alexandria but are owned by the same nationalised corporation. Gianaclis expands every year and the majority of the output goes for export. The firm also grows acres of geraniums from which oil is extracted for scent manufacture. A ton of these flowers produces one kilo of oil. A start is now being made in the production of olive oil and honey.

17. A pharaoh smiting his enemies as depicted on the wall of the Temple at Edfu

6 Aswan and Abu Simbel

Thanks to its delightful situation on the Nile and sunny, dry climate, Aswan has the same effect on the tourist as a glass of vintage wine; slightly heady, invigorating and to be savoured. The late Aga Khan, a connoisseur of enchanting places, chose it for his villa Nur el-Salaam (Light of Peace) and wished his mortal remains to lie at rest there. His wish has been fulfilled and his mausoleum stands high on the west bank of the Nile overlooking a most lovely and peaceful view.

In early days Aswan was a small trading post known as Suan (market) where the negro traders of the south met the merchants of ancient Egypt. From this small beginning it grew into a frontier town and year by year became more important, its riches increasing as trade between south and north flourished. It eventually became one of the wealthiest places in Pharaonic Egypt. No papyri tell of its population although it must have been large for it is recorded that at one time during a plague some 20,000 of its inhabitants died.

Aswan is always described as being close to the first 'cataract' – a word one usually associates with a waterfall. However the other dictionary definition is a rush of water through rocks or narrow defiles and the Nile traverses a number of these rapids formed of crystalline rock or sandstone. Generally the cataracts have numbers rather than names, the first being two or three miles upstream from Aswan and the numbers ascending as you go further from the sea. The town has been laid waste in turns by the Persians, Turks, Arabs and Nubians but nothing quelled its growth due to its strategic position. Shopping can be done in small stores or the native bazaar. The path from the old grain market merges into macadam roads crowded with cars plying to and fro between the luxury hotels.

You can drive through a pleasant maze of streets out beyond the town to see the old Aswan Dam and look down at the sluices through which water thunders. Far below in a wide expanse of swirling water there are tree-covered islets and great jagged rocks with bright green moss adhering to their sides. Away to the right the sun sparkles over Aswan. It is some distance away yet seems closer because of the clarity of the air. A mosque can be seen in the foreground behind which the town fans out with its labyrinth of buildings. Blue and white houses are interlaced with gardens and sycamore trees. It is difficult to remember that the little town nestling in this fertile curve of the Nile is surrounded by savage desert beyond which lies tropical Africa.

In complete contrast to the fury of the unleashed current, with its perpetual rainbow in the flying spray, the view from the opposite side of the bridge is of the calm lake of the reservoir. Here until recently temple pillars and pylons protruded above the water, the bulk of the buildings being submerged on the island of Philae which was inundated when the dam was built.

In Pharaonic times tradition held this island to be one of the burial places of Osiris. The ground was so sacred that only priests and temple attendants were allowed there to live. A number of religious plays were enacted each year including the mutilation, death and resurrection of Osiris. Great crowds were drawn annually to Philae for this religious ceremony and the island became known as the Pearl of Egypt.

In the early days of Christianity, Copts built two churches in honour of Saint Michael and Saint Athanasius on Philae, and remains of other churches as well as many Pharaonic temples have been excavated there down through the years.

No one thought then that the historic ruins and vaulted halls of the Isis temple, clustered about with palm groves and acacias, would be submerged and that fish would swim along the friezes, into the painted shrines and under the lintels.

However, the partially drowned monuments perhaps because of their great fame and beauty, still drew tourists. Boats could be hired to take visitors alongside the top of the pylons to see the carvings and try to glimpse the pillars below the surface.

Sir Ronald Storrs recalls in his book *Orientations* how he and Arthur Weigall, at the time Inspector-General of Upper Egypt, during one glorious sunset could not resist 'throwing off our clothes, diving into the Nile and coming up underneath the lintels into the dim painted shrines' where 'the sun reflected from the green water struck up against the gods and goddesses moving along the frieze . . . The animals turned this and that way, and the merry little god Bes danced once more for joy in the birth he personified.'

When the first Aswan Dam was built the temples were not completely submerged and during the summer, when the Nile was low, the water receded and half the pillars and much of the pylons could be seen. However with the building of the New High Dam the temples were in greater trouble than before. Their island lay between the two dams and would be subject to strong currents which would erode them and the water would drown them completely throughout the year. The Abu Simbel temples had been salvaged successfully and a new scheme was worked out to save those of Philae. With Unesco's backing, engineers have accomplished a remarkable feat. A coffer dam was built round the island and when this was completed the water was pumped out – at the rate of ten inches a day.

About the beginning of 1975 I was taken to see the work in progress We chugged out to the coffer dam, tied up to a wooden platform and climbed a ladder to the top where we stood on the rubble filling between the two rows of sheet piling which form the dam. A complete circle enclosed the island like an enormous pie-dish with corrugated edges. Below on flat grey soil stood the temples like miniature toys in a large bowl. Half a century in water had turned the walls from their once apricot colour to the same grey as the drowned island itself. Pumps were still working but much of the island was above the water line.

The steady pressure of the water on the temples over the years had not obliterated the bas reliefs of gods and goddesses. They remain, ghostlike, in stylized attitudes of giving and receiving gifts. A king was presenting a plump goose with spreading wings to Horus. And there was the chubby God Bes, as Sir Ronald had seen him years ago, still dancing to the music of his own lute. Columns of the interior court of the Isis temple still retain their decorative beauty unimpaired by years of inundation. The grey damp pillars of the charming little Graeco Roman kiosk, erected by Trajan and referred to as 'Pharaoh's Bed' due to its rectangular shape, are as elegant as ever. Save for the clicking of cameras everyone was silent as we gazed downward conscious that only ultra modern technology could have uncovered the lovely grey ghosts below. When the pumping has finished the temples will be carefully dismantled, the great blocks numbered and moved, piece by piece to the island of Hgiekia, a third of a mile away and completely safe from flooding. There they will be reassembled and probably, by the time this goes to print, visitors will once again be able to see the temples of Philae as they were at the turn of the century. Perhaps the palm groves and acacias will take some months to grow but the mimosa, lantana and other fast growing shrubs will soon be back. The monuments, baked once more by the sun, will shed their greyness and become as tawny as when David Roberts did his water colours of them more than a hundred years ago.

Two other islands in the Nile at Aswan which are 'musts' for visitors are Elephantine and Botanic Island. These are in no danger of flooding from the vast new Aswan Dam and can be easily reached by felucca.

It was from the shores of Elephantine that the Pharaohs of the fifth dynasty sprang. Not far from the first cataract it was referred to by the Egyptians in olden times as the Door to the South. Beyond the Egyptian border it was referred to as The Key to Egypt.

Elephantine was governed by a family of powerful nobles whose leader took the title Keeper of the Door of the South. They were very rich organisers of caravans and the Pharaohs entrusted their defence of that region to them. So strong were they that nobody dared rise against them and riches poured into their domain in the form of slaves, gold, ostrich feathers, ebony, skins and ivory. When barter was necessary it was a simple matter to procure granite from the Aswan quarries. The old Egyptian word for gold is nub and as the greatest quantity of gold for Egypt came from the south of the border the country there was known as Nubia.

During dynastic times the rainfall was plentiful on Elephantine. Fig trees and grape vines kept their leaves through the year. There is no such cultivation now yet the tourist can visualize some of the splendour of those remote days. Antiquities are always coming to light. In the Cairo Museum it is possible to see the strange mummified rams coated with gold which were excavated from Elephantine. The reason for these is extremely interesting.

The God Khnum was the deity of the First Cataract and a Sacred Ram was symbolic of the god on earth. The ram was selected from its fellows with as much care as is given to the Dalai Lama when he is chosen from the children of Tibet. The ram, attended by priests, then led a cloistered life in the temple. At death it was mummified and laid in a sarcophagus with the appropriate rites given to a Pharaoh. One horn and the tail were wrapped apart from the body. Gold encased the mummy and around its neck was hung a garland of bay leaves. It was believed that the sacred ram would eventually be reunited with Khnum in the life beyond life.

One of the best preserved Nilometers in Egypt is on the east bank of Elephantine. There are also many temple remains, obelisks and statues. If you go ashore near the Nilometer and climb some flights of steps to a walled garden, you will have a delightful surprise for the sprawling house within has been turned into a small museum. Facing you as you enter is a golden bust of Khnum with brown peaceful eyes. He is wearing a gold breast plate and shoulder straps.

These trappings once encased the mummy of a sacred ram. Five small rooms succeed each other filled with glass cabinets and cases of treasures from the Middle Kingdom. These include hand mirrors, scarabs, necklaces of amethyst the colours varying from mauve to deep purple, and others of cornelian and turquoise. Two unusual New Empire necklaces are of strung Hathor heads carved from turquoise. There are pieces of Byzantine jewellery, choakers, earrings, necklaces of garnets and other gems and several ivory combs, one being decorated with a baby giraffe and its mother. Once there was a large hallway behind the rooms but this has been turned into a gallery and is stacked with sarcophagi and mummy cases.

On the far western shore of the Nile from Elephantine Island a high elongated hill juts out into the river. There is a fringe of trees at the water's edge and near the summit a frieze of dynastic tombs. The hill's stark backbone is bare against the sky save for a small Sheik's tomb, the recently built dome adding to rather than detracting from the austere panorama.

The dynastic tombs, tier upon tier, are hewn out of the rock and open on to a terrace. They can be reached by climbing a steep staircase next to a sarcophagus slide, the latter looking like a deep ski run in the sand. These graves, cut into the thickest layer of stone near the top of the hill, were made for the rulers of Elephantine.

Botanic Island is often affectionately called 'Kitchener's Island' for it was presented to him when he was Consul-General in Egypt, and there he indulged his passion for flowers. He loved the island and ordered plants from India and all over the Middle and Far East. An enchanting place to visit it is now kept as a sort of botanical garden – a perfect place to end a day's sightseeing.

The way ashore is up a flight of steps edged with red hibiscus. An avenue of royal palm trees bisects the small island. Paths lead off this along herbaceous borders while blossoming trees give shade overhead. Poinsettias with red, pink and yellow flowers soar over one's head. There are large beds of purple castor beans, gerbera, asters, massive marigolds of flaunting coral and fragile tangerine birds of paradise. Masses of lantana of unusual colouring – not the ordinary yellow and brown variety – but clumps in shades of pink mauve and bright orange grow to enormous size and attract butterflies with gloriously tinted wings.

In the centre of the island there is an outdoor cafe with rustic seats and tables where you can have tea or soft drinks and buy beaded necklaces and other souvenirs. At sunset, fluttering birds agitate the leaves of the many different trees, eucalyptus, mimosa, flamboyants (the blossoms not the usual flame red but a rich golden yellow) and tropical shrubs from the Pacific. Your *felucca* will have sailed round the island and be waiting at the far side by the time you have wandered across.

Elephantine and Botanic Islands are not far apart and a third islet close by the latter has one of the most up to date hotels in Egypt, in a setting of trees and flower beds. It is cleverly designed with terraces and balconies overlooking the Nile and is managed by the same Oberoi group as the recently renovated Mena House near the Pyramids of Giza. Launches take you back and forth to the mainland every half hour.

The Hotel Aswan Oberoi with its 150 rooms, duplexes and luxury chalets can be regarded as a sunny, restful Shangri-La or as a centre of activity, according to the taste of the visitor. Plans are being made for a swimming pool, health club, yoga classes, tennis courts and a nine hole pitch and putt golf course. Duck shoots will be arranged from December to March with no limit on the bag. In the hotel's high tower, which gives fantastic views along the Nile, there will be an exclusive French restaurant with a Tzigane orchestra.

Thus Aswan is becoming a central point for sport as well as sightseeing. Many of Egypt's famous temples can be visited from the town such as Abu Simbel, Kom Ombo and Edfu. There will be return trips to Luxor and Karnak by air-conditioned buses as well as the usual boat trips along the Nile.

Of the hotels in Aswan none is better known than the Old Cataract Hotel so beloved by visitors between the two World Wars. Owned by the Upper Egypt Hotels Company it is rich in both beauty and atmosphere. With its reddish walls it stands on an ideal site sprawling along a granite bank in a curve of the Nile where the water is tranquil. The view from the roofed-over terrace high above the river at sunset is one of the most beautiful I have ever seen. Shimmering in the half light on the west bank and dovetailing into the landscape, is the mausoleum of the late Aga Khan. It is an exact copy of the small El Gyushi Mosque, a perfect example of early Moslem style on the Mokattam hills of Cairo.

The hotel has 200 bedrooms. The restaurant is a room within a room in the Arabic style, the inner walls pierced by arches from the floor to the ceiling which is inset with a coloured glass skylight covered with mushrabia work. The entrance to the hotel is through a large garden where, for the first time in my life, I saw poinsettias and roses blooming together.

The New Cataract Hotel shares the same 16 acre garden (which includes a swimming pool) and is under the same management. It also faces the Nile and has five storeys with 144 rooms (75 air conditioned) with bathrooms. The rooms are much smaller than in the old hotel but everything is thoroughly modern and there is a shop and hair dressing salon. Doctor Kissinger and his wife stayed here during the Middle East negotiations in the mid seventies.

A felucca can be hired from the hotel jetty to sail across the water to visit the Aga Khan's tomb. A winding roadway with a flight of shallow steps every few yards passes the Begum's villa on the way and there are several little sandstone benches where one can rest and admire the views.

The entrance to the mausoleum is up a gleaming rose granite staircase. Before you ascend you must remove your shoes. Large bronze doors swing back to reveal the mausoleum which is open to the sky. It is like a high courtyard with crenellated edging and is made of pinkish sandstone. The flooring is polished rose granite and thick red carpeting leads across it into a domed interior. Here lies a simple, pure white sarcophagus covered in Arabic script, the Aga Khan's tomb. Every day a small vase of fresh roses is placed on it. The Begum, when she is in residence at her villa, puts one rose there herself every day. To the right of the sarcophagus are two red cushions, one on the floor for the priest to sit on and the other to place behind his back against a pillar. A small wooden receptacle holds a Koran. Pilgrims come to pay homage from many parts of the world.

A short distance from the Aga's mausoleum there are ruins of an old Coptic monastery built during the twelfth century and dedicated to St. Simeon. The living quarters of the monks are still standing, as is part of the church.

Aswan granite is famed throughout the Middle East and visits to the quarries are arranged daily by the local tourist office and various hotels. Perhaps the best time to go on this tour is in the early morning because once you arrive there is no shade.

The countryside becomes rocky and bare near the quarries. Long ago obelisks were cut from this crystalline rock; one stands in New York, one before St. Peter's Cathedral in Rome, one in the Place de la Concorde in Paris and yet another Cleopatra's Needle in London. All were made during the imperial days of the Pharaohs and all were excavated from the Aswan quarries.

Your taxi will deposit you before a great expanse of sand intersected with mountainous pieces of glittering stratum. Hieroglyphic signs on stones tell where various sarcophagi and obelisks had been cut for different Pharaohs. Others show where steles and statues had been made. Most interesting perhaps is the 'unfinished' obelisk, a gargantuan piece of work some 92 feet long, which lies attached to a great mass of granite. You can walk along its length. No obelisk standing today is as long as this giant. During the eighteenth dynasty, while is was being wrought, it developed a large crack down one side. An attempt was made to cut it down to a smaller size but the massive piece of granite proved too flawed, the workmen were told to abandon the project, and ever since it has lain uncompleted in its crystalline bed.

Standing on the unfinished obelisk you can see over a wide stretch of the quarries. Great chunks of quartz sparkle in the sunshine, a variety of pinks, black and white. From this gleaming rock furnishings for the great Pharaonic temples emerged.

The cutting of the granite took long hours. Men patiently wedged wooden pegs into crevices and holes, then saturated them with water. As the wood expanded it cracked the quartz into required lengths. These pieces, some of them 200 feet long were brought to the Nile and floated in barges to various destinations. The granite covering the Pyramid of Mycerinus, the third Pyramid at Giza, was brought from Aswan in the fourth dynasty. The demand for this rosy granite still continues.

The building of the new High Dam about four miles upstream of the old town has formed a lake stretching far back into the Sudan. Should someone ask me what particular scene has filled me with awe during my lifetime without doubt I should reply, 'A few incredible minutes watching hordes of men and hundreds of machines building the Aswan High Dam, one of the largest man made structures in the world.' The site itself seemed unreal for I saw it for the first time at night. I felt as if I were standing on a high mountain gazing into an enormous valley below. Electric projectors shone down into deep fissures and crevasses where round the clock thousands of men burrowed into the living rock with bulldozers, cranes and gigantic automatic shovels. Toy-like lorries came and went, pin points of moving light twinkling in the deep inferno and the noise was deafening. Immense clouds of dust rose slowly from below to blot out the stars. The soft night air was laden with diesel fumes so that I could hardly breathe. Even so I had to remain a few minutes to watch the tiny ants below, the descendants of the men who built the Great Pyramid, building the modern wonder of today. At the peak period of the construction some 25,000 tons of rock were moved every 24 hours.

Even today the vast Lake Nasser has not reached its full extent. It will stretch from the first cataract to the third, a distance of some two hundred and fifty miles and this vast sheet of water will vary in width from fifteen to twenty miles. In years when the Nile is high this reservoir will store the excess water and at last the fellaheen will know exactly what water supplies they can expect for their sunbaked land and sow their three crops a year accordingly. In addition the generation of over two million kilowatts of electricity, by the passage of the water through the turbines in the power houses, means that Egypt is well placed for energy supplies.

Inevitably this enormous inundation caused concern to archaeologists and art lovers everywhere and several monuments have been moved to safe places. In 1962 the temple of Kalabsha, one of Nubia's largest ancient buildings, some 50 kilometres from Aswan, was dismantled by the German Archaeological Institute of Cairo. Dedicated to the god Mandulis about 27 B.C. it was built during the reign of Emperor Augustus over foundations of an earlier temple by Amenophis II and was associated with Isis, goddess of Philae. Later part of the building was converted into a church. The inaugural ceremony of the relocated 2000 year old temple was in March 1975 and its present site is on an island in Lake Nasser. The boat trip is a short one and you clamber up a hill to visit the temple which stands on a plateau.

A pylon, its decoration worn away, leads into an open court, girded on three sides by a colonnade, where there is a Nilometer 15 metres deep. The courtyard leads into a smaller one. In each the only decoration is on either side of the entrance but the columns retain their lotus and papyrus capitals. The three roofed over halls in the rest of the temple show the king worshipping and presenting gifts to gods and goddesses.

The view over Lake Nasser is spectacular from the temple roof but is even more dramatic if you follow the causeway leading from the temple to the much smaller one of Beit El Wali only five minutes walk distant. On the way stone benches are placed so that you may sit and enjoy the views. This monument, built by Ramses II and moved from Lower Nubia, has an open forecourt whose walls are cut with a series of reliefs giving details of the King's victories during the Nubian and Asiatic wars. The first one shows Ramses in his chariot drawn along by a prancing horse, his pet lion loping along beside him. He is in his traditional pose about to shoot an arrow.

The next scene shows Ramses under a canopy seated on his throne, receiving tributes of panther skins, myrrh, shields, ivory, ostrich feathers and ostrich eggs. More interesting are the gifts of live animals striding towards the throne. They include panthers, monkeys, ibexes, oxen and, most charming of all, a single giraffe.

From the forecourt you walk into a hall which is supported by slender fluted pillars. This in turn leads into the sanctuary which has two small niches each containing three statues cut out of the rock. These represent a deified Ramses flanked by two gods. The wall colouring in the sanctuary is remarkably fresh and might have been applied yesterday. Offerings are being presented to Ramses and gods whose bodies are of rosy hue. Their robes and jewellery are in vivid reds, blues and yellows. Such vivid colouring seems to bring the figures to life in this secluded spot. Even if you have little time to spare when visiting the island, try not to miss this small temple or the lovely views over the lake near its entrance.

Tourists arrive every day by bus and taxi to see the Nasser Lake and the great dam that created it. A double carriageway straddles the dam with flowering trees planted down the centre. On the downstream side a vast spout of water from the level controlling sluices bursts into hugh clouds of spray with a dancing rainbow in the centre. On the opposite side the blue water spreads as far as the eye can see, its surface sprinkled with millions of dancing sunbeams bright as diamonds. A short distance away steamers leave the new Port Sudan for Wadi Halfa.

Some 40 miles north of Wadi Halfa on the west shore of Lake Nasser stand the great temples of Abu Simbel on their new site. The Unesco operation moved not only the temple but also recreated the rock that framed it so that the reassembled monuments would appear in their natural setting. One hundred and fifty six tons of scaffolding were erected at the new location before the temple halls and chambers were pieced together again.

I have been fortunate in seeing the temples on their original site, then again while they were being dismantled and a third time in their new location. The temples are about 160 miles from Aswan and my first visit was by steamer from the little port of Shellal, some seven miles from Aswan airport.

We had arrived early in the afternoon, went straight aboard, and by teatime were on our way upstream. The food was simple but good. The round trip took three days and each afternoon there were freshly baked cakes for tea and at breakfast hot croissants.

Night comes quickly in Egypt, but although it was November, the air was warm and dry. Searchlights were switched on either side of our ship as soon as it became dark and we could see the river banks almost as plainly as by day.

Next morning after breakfast we passed by many small villages and watched the fellaheen busy at work; children going to school, animals grazing off scrubb and meagre grass or turning waterwheels. Men on donkey-back guided their beasts, which had no bridle, by the aid of a little stick which they held against its neck whenever they wished to turn right or left. As the heat of the day intensified grazing animals made for the shade of the many thorn trees. Flights of exotic birds disturbed by our ship winged over the water. Villages gave way to apricot sand shelving up to bare brown hills with a background of washed blue sky.

It was in the evening, less than 30 hours after we left Shellal, that our searchlights picked out the lovely temple of Nefertari in the darkness on the west bank of the Nile. The facade some 84 feet long, is ornamented with six tall statues of Ramses II and his beautiful wife Nefertari – each with the left leg forward as if they were striding towards us straight into the river.

The scene was like a brightly lit stage set. In the foreground the acacia trees in full bloom threw lacy patterns before the feet of the colossi. There were several tents beneath the acacia trees and men appeared out of them and ran down to help the sailors moor our ship.

Our guide led us ashore. Clad in cotton slacks and low shoes, we followed like a school crocodile across the sand, which was still warm from the heat of the day and yielded with each step we took. We passed the facade of the temple and came to more acacia trees. How the acacia exists in the dry sand is a mystery yet it plays a role in the life of the Egyptian – both ancient and modern. The pods can be made into ink and blue dye, its gum – gum arabic – is valuable, the bark contains tannin and its wood (in a country where trees are few) is hard and almost imperishable. It flourishes along the Nile in Upper Egypt and besides its many uses its canary yellow flowers could not be prettier or more fragile.

Suddenly we could see the temple of Abu Simbel. It was further back on the desert shore than the other, yet was so much larger that it appeared to be equally close to the river. One imagines any great building cut out of the living rock to be high above the waterline. One of the surprises of Abu Simbel was how extremely close the vast temple was to the river. If one of the colossal figures of Ramses II had got up from its sitting position, with two mighty steps the Pharaoh could stride into the Nile. It was easy to believe that these statues were of the illustrious Ramses, the Pharaoh who lived 1333 years before Christ, one of the greatest builders of all time, a liberal patron of the arts and sciences and the noted warrior who subjugated Nubia and Mesopotamia.

Searchlights had been arranged on the vast sand apron before the temple and we could see perfectly. We were led into the temple where more arc lights lit up the interior which was hewn out of solid sandstone to a depth of some 185 feet. We found ourselves in a large hall where eight figures of Ramses dressed as Osiris, about 17 feet high reached into the vaulting. The ceiling was marvellously decorated. Between the second and third statues on either side there was a delightful plump goose of red and brown, its tail feathers folding into each other perfectly. The whole of the left wall depicts Ramses' battle with the Hittites at Kadesh with great panoramic affect. The most charming relief is of the Pharaoh in his war chariot with his pet lion trotting by his side.

We followed our guide into a second great hall, this time with four elaborately carved pillars – then a third hall off which opened three chambers – the centre one being the Holy of Holies. The temple had been built facing the east so that the early rays of the rising sun at the equinoxes should penetrate the whole length of the building until they rested on the four figures in the innermost sanctuary. Judging by giant hinge recesses, pointed out by our guide, there had been a double door leading to it. None dared enter this retreat or open the sacred portals except the Pharaoh and his High Priest. Although no priest had worshipped there for 3000 years the atmosphere was such that when we talked it was in whispers. We looked at the four figures. Time had dealt less kindly with them than the colossi outside. Nevertheless, their tranquil dignity had not been impaired. They were seated, a little larger than life-size, and regarded us calmly. How magnificent they must have been during Ramses' lifetime. Then they had been whole and magnificently coloured; the first two (Harmachis and Ramses himself) were red, the third (the Sun God Amen-Ra) blue and the fourth (Ptah, Patron God of the arts) white. Before the figures there was a sacrificial stone where long ago the sacred barque of the Pharaoh had been placed.

We walked out into the warm night and across the sand dunes to the Nefertari temple and went inside. Once again arc lights showed up the murals to advantage. Not many war scenes met our eyes. The background of the reliefs were faintly pink and golden – the features of the love goddess Hathor rounded and feminine, the hair style strangely modern. Delicate carvings in pastel shades portrayed Nefertari as beautiful as Nefertiti. Her royal robes were cut on simple lines, sometimes of the finest linen or transparent lawn – the long skirts with knife-edge pleating. One lovely picture shows Nefertari presenting offerings to Anuket, Goddess of the First Cataract, the latter wearing an enchanting crown resembling a lotus flower.

That night I sat on deck and looked at Nefertari's temple. It was almost as brilliantly illuminated as day by the ship's searchlights. The men who lived in the tents took advantage of the light on the sand apron. One little group played noughts and crosses in the sand, another built a small fire and made tea. The remainder just sat in circles and discussed the affairs of the day.

I went ashore the following morning while it was still dark to watch the sun rise on Abu Simbel. The air was fresh but cool and I was glad I had pulled on a sweater before leaving the ship.

The two jutting walls protecting the larger temple from encroaching sand were in shadow. It was not really dark. The sky was a bright sapphire and there was a boat-shaped moon. To the left of the temple the planet Venus still shone brightly. The sky on the horizon became a faint pink which gradually melted into green and spread over the water. Soon sunrays fingered the sky and turned the pink to orange. As the light grew stronger the summit of the temple turned a rich golden colour and the large handsome features of the Pharaoh were uncovered. The eyes stared straight into the rising sun, and I noticed that the eyeballs protruded in such a way that when the sun was full on them they appeared to be alive. Shadows fell away as the sun climbed down the dignified 65-foot figures of the Pharaoh until it revealed the charming little statues of the beautiful Nefertari and his children alongside his mighty legs. Birds began to twitter and flew busily in and out of the deep carvings in the stonework. I joined several other passengers from the ship who had now come ashore and went inside the temple. Sunlight slanted in through the high entrances turning the Osiris figures of Ramses golden. Only when the ship's gong sounded for breakfast did any of us realise it was 7.30 a.m.

Four years later I visited Abu Simbel again, this time by hydrofoil. We left Shellal at dawn and arrived five hours later. Hydrofoils can do the round trip in twelve hours and are a luxurious way for tourists to travel as they are air conditioned and meals are served on board.

We were all tense with excitement to see the final stages of the salvage operation and clambered ashore and along a path which led to a huge cofferdam. This fanned in front of the temples and we walked along its rim. The bright sunlight caused people not wearing sunglasses to screw up their eyes as

we stared down into the great trough which had housed the
larger of the temples. Small, half-naked figures were busily
working below us.

We could not look away from the huge deep cavity where
the Ramses temple had been. Gigantic scars criss-crossed the
far side where the engineers had to excavate almost 190 feet
down through the cliff behind the temple before they could
start cutting it into moveable blocks. Then the great chunks
had been carefully lifted onto trucks and taken to a selected
spot high on another cliff safely out of reach of the rising
water. All that remained in the huge pit below us was a
portion of the temple base and the enormous feet of one of
Ramses' statues. Holes had already been drilled in the feet
and the lifting bars had been inserted. This same process was
used for all the blocks as it had been decided before lifting
began that they might not stand up to the strain of encircling
cables. A further precaution against damage was that plastic
resin had been sprayed over all surfaces to protect the porous
sandstone from disintegrating when cutting began. The blocks
were cut with hand saws, some of them wire, others diamond
toothed which had been specially designed for the task.

The structure beneath the Pharaoh's feet had been marked
off into square blocks for removal, each painstakingly
numbered. In all 950 pieces were moved.

A cloud of sand drew our attention from the work below as
a truck lumbered just behind us. After the air cleared we went
to see how the Nefertari temple excavations were getting on.
The story was the same. Another gaping cavity showed where
the smaller temple had been and the actual foundation which
remained was being measured into blocks and then painted
with numbers before the task of cutting began.

We then walked over to some waiting jeeps and were driven
up a winding hill to see the new site for the temples – some two
hundred and ten feet above the original level of the river.

We stepped out on what appeared to be a flat plateau. Some
distance beyond were the living quarters of the men who
worked on the site. Rows of houses were girded with small
plots of grass and flower beds. There were one or two shops

and, most amazing of all in such an arid spot, a swimming pool!

Stretching far in front of us there appeared to be a giant's cemetery with great 30-ton headstones. It was impossible to believe that these enormous slabs were to be dovetailed together to rebuild the Abu Simbel temples – yet this was being done. Walking through a forest of scaffolding we entered chambers which had been reassembled from the larger temple.

Semi-darkness engulfed us. As our eyes grew accustomed to the lack of light the wall reliefs could be discerned and welcome coolness crept about us. We came to a chamber only partially finished and open to the sky. I looked closely at the walls but the joins could not be seen. This was understandable when I watched a man pushing what appeared to be a little gauze into a tiny crevice with the precision of a dentist, in order to fill it.

Perhaps the most fascinating moments were when we strolled among the great blocks of masonry. It was unusual to be able to study coloured reliefs in full daylight. Indeed, some of the murals were so fragile in colouring that they were protected by rush screens from the bleaching sunshine.

How strange an experience it was to walk up to one of the great faces of Ramses and look straight into it. The upper part of the eyeballs were curved to give the correct perspective when the face is atop its sixty five foot figure and viewed from below. The Pharaoh's ears had been separated from the faces. I drew close to one. The hole in the pierced lobe was so large I could have put my foot through it!

My last visit to see the temples was fascinating indeed. Despite the fact that their removal to the new site had cost £15 million is it almost impossible to believe that they had ever been anywhere else. To see them from the air is an unforgettable sight. You fly over the open desert along Lake Nasser and circle over the temples. The great statues of Ramses stare out over the lake with their sphinx like expressions as if they had never moved.

There are two differences about the larger of the two

temples. To one side of the Hittite stele an Englishman lies buried. When the temple was being moved to its present site a coffin was uncovered and the mummified figure of an English major in uniform was found. A plaque on the coffin related that he was Major Tideswell and that he had died on the march against the Mahdi in 1884. Research revealed relations in England who were informed. The Tideswell family felt it fitting that the Major's body should remain where it had rested for so many years and it was reinterred next to the Hittite stele.

To the far right of the entrance there is a door which appears to go into the hillside. It leads into a false mountain. In reality this is an enormous reinforced concrete dome, probably the largest in existence, which enfolds the temple. It is 80 feet high and 200 feet across at the base. Over the top of it sand and gravel has been spread to a depth of 6-10 feet so that, when viewed from the outside, it presents the appearance of a natural mountain. It is a wonderful feat of engineering fitted with strain gauges and pendula to indicate any movement or subsidence. The contrast between one aspect of thousands of years ago presented outside and the ultra modern, stark, functional interior, both in the middle of the desert, is astonishing.

Imagine complete isolation from road and rail in a sunny, dry climate. Imagine a comfortable hotel with all mod con even to a swimming pool close by but in the desert with at present the only approaches by air or water. Away from it all and, were it not for one of the largest man-made lakes in the world, an oasis. It is what Las Vegas must once have been like only endowed with natural advantages. Fresh vegetables and fruit are flown in daily to the hotel or come by boat from Aswan and grilled fish from the lake is delicious. The bar has a Nubian flavour with colourful basketwork and lights festooned with native-made glass medallions. For the visitor there is plenty to do – fishing, swimming and sunbathing besides visiting one of the world's most fantastic antiquities. It is of course Abu Simbel and the hotel appropriately is called the Nefertari.

7 Luxor

The name Luxor is a corruption of the Arabic word Al-Uksur meaning 'the palaces' and for some 15 centuries that is what it was – a leading city of ancient Egypt full of palaces. The Greeks gave it the name Thebes and told of its splendour, of its pink granite obelisks capped with gold, temple doors plated with electrum, richly painted columns and forecourts covered with sheets of silver. The original city has completely disappeared but two of its temples remain which even the frightful destruction in the seventh century by Assurbanipal failed to raze.

Modern Luxor is a thriving little town, its main street, edged with trees, being a delightful corniche road along the Nile with flights of steps running down to small landing stages. Hotels line the opposite side.

The airport is some seven miles north east of the town and the drive to your hotel is a pleasant one through a farming area with shady canals. When I arrived on the outskirts of the town recently it was to be driven through a parade. Several local people were going on pilgrimage to Mecca and to see them off at Luxor railway station masses of townspeople, as well as friends and relations, were in festive mood to give them a cheerful farewell. Camels were draped with colourful lengths of cloth edged with sequins, their heads decorated with old electric bulbs. Little girls had donned their best dresses of lurex and lamé which glittered in the sunlight. Bands marched along accompanied by dancing children and grown-ups keeping time to the music. Donkeys trotted by, their bridles gay with woollen tassles. Men and women chanted and sang and their happiness was so infectious that even the airport taxi drivers blew their horns, not just to get through the crowds but to keep time with the music.

When I had unpacked at the New Winter Palace Hotel I walked out onto my balcony to see the view across the river where bare yellow hills melted into the blue sky. Down in the street people were returning from the parade. Flat horse-drawn carts carried the women folk in batches of six and eight, homeward. They looked like nuns in their black robes and veils save that they sat cross legged. The children seemed tireless but the bandsmen sauntered along slowly gesticulating with their instruments as they talked to friends.

Later in the afternoon I went for a sail in a felucca with other guests from the hotel. Nothing is more peaceful than gliding along the Nile at Luxor just before sunset – unless it is at Aswan. Everything was quiet and fish leaped high from the water. Birds winged their way back to the trees as the sun sank lower and lower. Colours faded into each other until a pale lilac and coral spread from the sky to the water. As we arrived back at the landing stage the Theban Hills on the west bank of the Nile were shrouded in a misty greyness and then vanished from sight.

Most of the Luxor hotels can be reached from the river by going ashore at the nearest jetty and walking across the tree-edged corniche. As in Aswan there is an 'Old' and a 'New' Cataract Hotel so in Luxor there is an 'Old' and a 'New' Winter Palace Hotel. The buildings are also similar and belong to the same Upper Egypt Hotels Company. The 'Old' Winter Palace has always been known for its beautiful garden and lately a swimming pool has been added. The 'New' Winter Palace has everything for the tourist's comfort. Its 144 rooms have bathrooms and air conditioning. The shutters and windows instead of having to be swung back, slide into recesses. There are other innovations such as phosphorescent light switches and shoe drawers beneath luggage racks. The decor is ultra modern but retains the lotus as the main motif, even in the deep pile carpeting. There is a very good restaurant.

Tourists come to the town in increasing numbers not only by rail and air – Egypt Air have daily flights from Cairo – but also by Nile steamer. If you travel by the latter route it is very exciting as you come along the river to watch the columns of Luxor temple rise into view. Their enormous lotus blossom capitals seem to hold their heads up to the sun and, beyond them and the town itself, the countryside stretches flat and richly green. As you step ashore onto a landing stage it is in all probability where Antony stepped ashore in the days of Cleopatra.

Sightseeing is a pleasure even for those very young and old visitors who tire easily. It is possible to enjoy a short jaunt and then rest or have tea at one of the nearby hotels while waiting for other members of sightseeing parties who have ventured forth on more prolonged expeditions.

Shopping is something to be looked forward to at Luxor. Perhaps the most interesting thing to buy is alabaster as it is quarried nearby and is cheaper here than in the larger cities. The ornaments, vases and bowls vary in colour from deep apricot to palest amber. You can get hollow lamps with lights inside them to show off the grain of the alabaster. Then of course there are the antiquities, some genuine most of them not, some large, some small. For generations it has been as natural for the local fellaheen to search in the sand for antiquities, when he has a moment to spare from his fields, as it is for us to pick wild flowers. Professor Bryan Emery told me that during the twenties, after Howard Carter had discovered Tutankhamen's tomb, small antiquities became so popular for tourists that one particular merchant would offer new caps to local peasants if they would first fill them with scarabs. It is not so easy to pick up scarabs today. I love a recent story about an elderly merchant who was asked if his scarabs were genuine. 'Of course!' he ejaculated 'I make them in my own kitchen.'

Scarabs are made in just the same way as in the past. Perhaps one could argue that it is as interesting to have a modern one made by a living artist as an ancient one.

Although at Luxor the climate is perfection itself and most

types of sport can be had for the asking, it is the two great temples, Luxor and Karnak, that draw the tourists. Luxor temple was built during the time of the New Empire, more than 1000 years before Christ. At its completion it sprawled on the bank of the Nile in a maze of columned halls, colonnades, chambers and courts and was considered the most beautiful monument in the whole of Egypt.

Temples were designed in such a way that succeeding Pharaohs by adding to them, enhanced their beauty. As through one thousand years a redwood sapling grows into a three hundred foot giant, so through the centuries Pharaonic temples expanded into grandiosity.

The creator of Luxor temple, Amenophis III, was well called the Magnificent. During his reign of 35 years he lavished most of his gold, not on war and conquest, but on sculpture and temples. Egypt was at the height of her imperial power and the city obelisks literally glittered with gold. The Pharaoh spent much of his time studying architectural designs. He was responsible for the Great Court and the Hall of Columns – the latter indeed was the first project of its kind ever attempted.

Two reigns later Ramses II added another courtyard with porticoes, two obelisks, a pylon, a large colonnade and many gargantuan statues.

Before entering the monument you must look at the magnificent pylon. Scrolled across the facade is the history of the battle of Kadesh, the great victory Ramses won over the Hittites on the Orontes in 1300 B.C. A colossus of the Pharaoh, built from a single block, is placed with its back to the pylon close to the entrance and on the opposite side stands another and an obelisk whose fellow was taken to Paris in 1833 and erected where the guillotine once reared its ugly head – in the Place de la Concorde.

At one time tall flagpoles, emerging from hollow passages up through the pylon, streamed with pennants on festive occasions. As you cross over the threshold of the great doorway you will notice a deeply carved winged disc in the lintel.

Many years ago before the temple was excavated a village had been built within its protecting colonnades. When it had crumbled nobody cleared away the rubbish and a new one was built over the rubble. Through the years the temple gradually vanished from sight and during the fourteenth century a mosque, built by a religious man named Abu Hagag, was actually high above the site of the great courtyard of Ramses II. The mosque was revered because Abu Hagag was a descendant of a saint who lived in Mecca during the lifetime of Mohammed. When the temple was excavated the villagers were rehabilitated outside its walls but the mosque was left, held aloft in the high columns like a bird's nest.

As you enter the temple through the pylon today you suddenly see the Abu Hagag mosque high in the columns above on the left. The little mosque perched above the temple is not so very much out of place. If you are lucky you will see the muezzin come out on to the slender minaret and call the faithful to prayer, his ringing voice a link between the worship of the old gods and that of the God of all – a link from ancient to modern Egypt.

Beyond the mosque 11 red granite statues of the Pharaoh gaze fixedly ahead between pillars which surround the court. Each effigy of the King has one foot placed forward as if walking, the mighty hands are clenched, the massive bodies nude save for knee length pleated skirts. As at Abu Simbel, behind and to the left of several statues stands a small replica of Ramses' Queen, Nefertari.

Time has dealt more gently with one of these little Queens than with the Pharaoh. She is very beautiful. Her luxuriant thick plaits fall beneath her head covering to her breast, her rounded face shows no lines of worry. Her full moulded mouth curves in the suspicion of a smile. She looks happy and at the same time demure – as befits the Queen of a God.

Many of the temple reliefs show the splendour of the processions which took place along the paved avenue of ram headed sphinxes between Luxor and Karnak. Pharaoh is shown distributing figs, dates, pomegranates and other fruits to the people on the route. Most delightful is an elongated frieze of a line of dancing girls, gliding with rhythmical steps in honour of the King. Each girl is bent as far back as the knees of the girl behind her with such elasticity that you wonder why the minute supple figures do not swing upright again. Semi-nude acrobats are turning somersaults. Music is playing and the whole populace is gay, for it is festival time when Pharaoh munificently bestows favours on his people, happy in the knowledge he is one with Amen-Ra the patron God of Thebes.

The approach to the temple's main court is along a magnificent colonnade of seven pairs of gigantic pillars, the famous Hall of Columns. They rise 42 feet into the air, topped with papyrus blossoms whose filaments flatten out at the summits to support heavy blocks of architrave, placed horizontally from pillar to pillar. The columns soar heavenward like two lines of giant redwood trees, but instead of the darkness thrown by interwoven branches in primeval forests, sunlight streams down their sides and casts shadows over the floor like lengths of purple carpeting.

The main court of Amenophis III covers a vast area and is surrounded with double aisles of columns in the form of bunches of tied papyrus of the 'bud' variety. The reliefs are deeply incised.

You continue on through a maze of chambers. The temple has been torn down in places, changed and rebuilt. In one court Alexander had ordered four columns dismembered and replaced them with a square mass of masonry which was then carved with frescoes. One shows the God of Fertility receiving wine.

During the fourth century Christians turned part of the temple into a church and you can see the religious pictures painted over Pharaonic reliefs. In this ancient pagan temple Christianity and Islam meet, for the mosque of Abu Hagag is not far distant.

Once a thousand ram headed sphinxes, each holding a replica of Pharaoh Amenophis III between its paws, linked the temples of Luxor and Karnak together by an avenue a mile and a half long. It began from the banks of the Nile. Along the river route, nobles and their retinues approached the temple in many oared boats bedecked with gorgeous tapestry. While they dropped their great sails at the mooring stages other craft went by, laden with gold, ivory and ostrich feathers from Nubia. What superb sights their crews must have seen. Karnak covered four hundred acres by the riverside. Brilliant painting adorned its walls, while from its high entrance four flags fingered the sky. Steles of lapis lazuli were set on both sides of the foremost pylon, of which there were ten in all, and vast quantities of malachite, silver and gold covered the facade with inlay work. Amenophis's royal architect of the same name had set up a colossus of the Pharaoh hewn from gritstone, which soared some 67 feet in the air. The gates and columns were covered with gold while the gleam of silver could be glimpsed from the floors within. Obelisks towered over all, glittering with metal in the sunlight. Formal gardens fanned out either side from the Avenue of Sphinxes. A fabulous sight by day it must have seemed a paradise by moonlight so that from the river even the miserable captives on board military ships forgot their wretchedness when they saw the peerless Karnak. The temple took over 2800 years to build and tourists owe much of what they see today to Amenophis III.

The Pharaoh's head architect drew plans for a magnificent hall which would cover 6,000 square yards, the most famous of all hypostyle halls ever conceived. It had 134 columns, many 70 feet in height and exceeding 20 feet in circumference. All were covered with decorations and inscriptions in vivid colouring. The hall was roofed over and the sun shone through stone fretted openings high in the nave on either side. The mightiest columns culminated in soaring full-flowering lotus blossoms. Other columns were topped with massive lotus buds, typifying the closed flower at night.

Today, beyond the remains of this majestic hall, deeply incised reliefs can be glimpsed up to the top of a slender obelisk. It is the remaining obelisk of two ordered by Queen Hatshepsut. She commanded they should be ready within seven months. They were quarried from Aswan and carved with inscriptions embellished with gold and silver so that they should 'be seen from a great distance'. The royal edict fulfilled they were placed, 105 and 98 feet high respectively, in a rectangular hall where the oracle of Amen had named her first husband King. Hatshepsut's second husband Thothmes III hated the powerful Queen to such a degree he ordered that not only should her name be erased from the temples, but that her pictures should be obliterated and her statues torn down. Yet at Karnak this single obelisk escaped and is a lasting memorial to a great queen who like Amenophis III, abhorred war and encouraged the arts of peace.

Added to the genius of Amenophis III were the riches bestowed on Karnak by Thothmes III, gleaned from seventeen Asian invasions. Far Eastern plants bloomed in the formal gardens and were copied by artists who carved them in bas reliefs so that, instead of the usual reeds, wild fowl gracefully fluttered up amongst exotic tropical flowers.

In one of these open courts built by Ramses III there is the usual array of statues that one associates with this Pharaoh, but the figures mingle with the columns in a different guise. Although representations of Ramses they are in mummy raiment, symbolic of Osiris. Hands holding the sceptre and whip are crossed outside funerary linen. Despite the immensity of the statues and the fact that they are open to the sky the court is weighed down with the solemnity of death.

The circuit of Karnak is over two and a half miles long, astonishingly grandiose. For one day's visit it is advisable to study a plan of the temple first and decide what interests you most.

One of the most delightful places is a small rectangular chamber which contains two god statues, a male and a female. These are so graceful it is not surprising to learn that they had been presented to the temple by King Tutankhamen – the only trace of his beneficence in the temple. One of himself and the other his wife.

In one of the three halls of Seti stands a figure of Ramses II, enormous and mutilated – yet splendid. Much is missing. Archaeologists work at the jigsaw puzzle of piecing broken masonry together year after year. The fragments lying around today will become fewer and fewer as they resume their rightful places. The very foundations are complex, having been sunk different ways during various reigns; salt currents in the soil have caused much damage and the varying levels of the Nile from year to year have weakened the bases of many columns. Despite the difficulties reconstruction work is carried on and future generations will see more and more of the temple restored and perhaps the formal gardens edging the Avenue of Sphinxes glowing once again with flowers.

Many of the reliefs are complete and as strikingly beautiful as when they were first finished. One which gives particular pleasure is of Ramses offering sacrifices to Amen. Beneath the Pharaoh are seven quite perfectly carved unguent jars, rounded and beautifully shaped, so real it seemed strange that the air is not laden with sweet fragrance. Each jar symbolised seven years of the Pharaoh's reign.

Most thought provoking at Karnak is the sacred lake. It is artificial and was sunk during the reign of Thothmes III. Its level varies, as in a Nilometer, by infiltration from the river. The water looks fathomless although it is not very deep. Faint white lines of brine at the edging of the stone quay betray the presence of salt. On a high square plinth at one corner of the lake crouches a gargantuan granite scarab, still guarding the sacred stretch of water.

During the migratory season the lake is covered by birds of all kinds. Probably wild fowl were netted from these very waters during Pharaonic times, for cages of wild birds were one of the most impressive gifts to be offered to the gods.

You can go down stone steps at the little quayside which edges into the water, down the same steps which priests descended when they reverently lowered royal cedar barges with the bodies of dead Pharaohs. The barges encircled the sacred lake seven times before being lifted out and taken to the Valley of the Kings.

There are those who visit Luxor and, having seen the lavishness of its two temples, will not travel further afield, refusing to believe that other monuments could equal the splendour they have already seen. Certainly Luxor and Karnak merit numerous visits for it is impossible to appreciate their many wonders in a day. You not only see glorious shrines but sense the fantastic power of the Pharaohs whose absorbing passion in building, however catholic their tastes, was for sheer size and massiveness. It is not easy to decide which is the more beautiful, Luxor or Karnak, but Karnak wins as far as size is concerned, for it is the most spacious monument of its kind in the world.

It is difficult to imagine exactly what the city of Thebes was like. It acted as a setting not only for the temples of Karnak and Luxor but for the other great mortuary temples whose remains still lie in the western plain near the Valley of the Kings. But an illusion brings 'The hundred-gated Thebes' of Homer back to life when you visit the Son et Lumiere performance at Karnak temple in the evening. The illusion is further enhanced if you do not go by taxi but take a horse and carriage from your hotel. This is the traditional way to visit the temple even in daylight. Your carriage will be joined by many others as you clip-clop along the corniche.

Lights beneath the paws of the lines of ram sphinxes light the pathway into the temple where, standing among the brightly illuminated pillars, you can listen to the story of Karnak from the beginning. Pools of darkness soften blemishes and vivid lighting brings reliefs to a liveliness never seen by day. Even in November the heat of the day still rises from the sand and stone at your feet so that you remain warm. Coloured lights brighten and dim, scenes come and go, the voices change and there is music. You move with the spellbound audience further and further into the temple. Later the lighting and voices lead to an open amphitheatre behind the sacred lake where there are rows of seats. You remain here until the end of the performance.

Finally the lights dwindle, the voices recede and the music dies away. Only the granite scarab on his plinth remains watchful. Gradually your eyes adjust to the moonlight and you can make your way back to your carriage.

8 The Fantastic Valley of the Kings

It is wise to see the temples of Luxor before visiting the Valley of the Kings, for they reveal the fixation each Pharaoh had with his death. Realizing this the visitor can readily grasp the reason for mummification. To enable him to decipher the tombs' richly painted walls (in a cemetery that once held not only the royal dead, but one of the greatest treasure troves of all times) it is useful to have an idea of what the ancient Egyptians believed the after-life held for them.

The macabre art of embalming reached its peak of perfection at Thebes. It was practised and known in Egypt for at least 5,000 years, being discontinued some 500 years after the birth of Christ. Those following this calling joined special guilds which were appointed by law.

Mummifying was done in three different ways. The most skilful method, and therefore very expensive, was by extracting the brain through the nose with a special iron probe, without disfiguring the face in any way, and removing the intestines through the side after an incision had been made with a sharp instrument. The body's cavity was filled with cassia, myrrh and other fragrant substances, then sewn together and laid in natron (sesquicarbonate of soda) for 70 days. After being carefully washed it was finally wrapped in strips of fine linen and smeared with gum. According to the historian, Diodorus, this cost a talent of silver – the equivalent of over 700 Egyptian pounds today.

The second method was far less complicated. The entrails were dissolved, the brain not removed and the body laid in natron for 70 days. This procedure was half the price of the first and dispersed all save skin and bones.

The third method was commonly used for it cost little money and was merely injecting a strong astringent into the body and salting it for 70 days.

If the internal organs were mummified they were separated, washed in palm oil and powdered with aromatic herbs, after which they were sealed in four jars. One held the heart and the others the liver and the two intestines. The jars were made of alabaster or terracotta and each was inscribed. The god to whom each was dedicated protected it.

They were buried with the mummy together with small ushabti figures, glazed faience statues, who would assist the mummy in the underworld. Amulets were placed round the neck of the dead, amongst them the papyrus sceptre, emblem of the youth hoped for in the next world; the vulture, ensuring the protection of Isis; the buckle, a small red stone symbolic of the blood of Isis; the Key of Life; and the utchat in the form of an eye, the sign for good health and happiness. Other sacred things protected the body including scarabs, ornamented with the deceased adoring Osiris, and modelled index and middle fingers representing the two fingers of Horus stretched out to aid the dead.

As soon as a man died he became identified with Osiris for it was supposed that this god had been the first to be embalmed and that Anubis had been head embalmer.

It was believed that the dead traversed a long, lonely river called the Tuat before attaining the glory of Ra. The Tuat, which was neither below nor above the level of Egypt, had its beginning on the west bank of the Nile, ran north, then bent around to the east and ended where the sun rose. It was divided into 12 parts beginning and ending with a chamber. The name of the entrance chamber was Amentet, which was a place of twilight. As the deceased continued the awful journey the darkness became completely black. Many were the horrible monsters and hideous reptiles that rose from the depths of boiling water. The last sections gradually lightened until the final chamber, a replica of Amentet, was reached.

Ra, or Amen-Ra as the god was called at Thebes, made his

18. *The tops of the temple of Philae projecting from the water before the High Dam was built*

19. *The temple surrounded by the coffer-dam preparatory to its removal*

way safely through the terrible ordeals. Each dawn the god emerged triumphantly from the Tuat and the light from his raiment flooded the earth. If the deceased secured a passage in the god's sacred barge, his safety was assured. At midnight the souls of mummies were judged by Osiris after which the worthy continued the journey with Amen-Ra, and rose with him over the earth in renewed life and happiness. The wicked were annihilated.

The priests taught the faithful the various divisions of the Tuat and where the worst dangers threatened by the aid of pictures and knowledge gleaned from the Book of the Dead. They presided over the construction of royal tombs and saw to it that the subterranean passages joining the chambers and halls resembled the long narrow valley of death.

Inscriptions painted on the walls of the tombs are grouped thus:

A The Book of the Praisings of Ra which contains 75 paragraphs of the 75 names of Ra with a different attribute to each.
B The Book of Gates. This gives the 12 names of the various gates on the Tuat and what must be done at each one.
C The Book of the Underworld, which gives knowledge for the deceased of the greatest importance. For instance, it describes the kingdom of the god Seker and the terrible serpents guarding it where darkness is never pierced and the depths never known.

The burial ceremonies were symbolic of the after life, the body being borne on a boat in the funeral procession. This was dragged on a sled by oxen. Milk was sprinkled before it to lay the dust. Priests read funerary chants and burnt incense. Mourners wailed, garbed in blue grey garments, and behind them followed servants and slaves carrying furniture, chests of jewellery, chariots, food and all the impedimenta that was to be buried with the deceased.

At the tomb dancers and musicians awaited the mummy,

20. *The Step Pyramid at Sakkara*
21. *A view from the Pyramid of Cheops towards the Pyramid of Chephren at Giza*

which, on arrival, was placed upright for the ceremony called the Opening of the Mouth. Very little is known of this save that priests intoned formulae and offerings were held before the deceased. The body was then placed in its final resting place.

The priests emerged from the vaults chanting sacred words. All had been accomplished that would ensure safety for the departed soul in the after life. One day the mummy would be reincarnated, in the meantime it rested in pomp and splendour. Yet the Ka, the indestructible spirit, was free to pass from the mummy to the gods and back again. It is sometimes pictured as a human-headed bird. This divine part carried on the mummy's life in the tomb. It worked, found pleasure, ate and drank, a personality without form, sensuous yet divine. The lavishness of the tomb had to be such that the Ka could live and move with enjoyment. To ensure nothing would be touched by human hands the sepulchre had to be hidden from human eyes.

In addition to the Ka there were three counterparts of the mummy: the Sahu, the waiting immortal body; the Khaib, or shadow; and the Ab, the ghost of the heart.

A small furnished tomb provided enough space for ordinary folk and their Kas, but in the case of Pharaohs who in life had lived in great palaces, the final resting place had to be sumptuous. As soon as a king came to the throne, plans for his burial vault were submitted, and when accepted, work began immediately. As year succeeded year, the tomb grew in splendour.

Unfortunately entombment, especially royal entombment, went hand in hand with robbery. There were always those who were prepared to risk the loss of their souls if, during their human existence, they could have untold riches.

Thothmes I, fearful that his own tomb should suffer from grave robbers as had his forefathers in their royal pyramids, broke with the pyramid tradition and arranged in secret with his head architect, Ineni, that his vault should be burrowed deep into the yellow cliffs of Thebes. It was commissioned to be as pretentious as any pyramid before it. Later Pharaohs followed suit. Such fantastic undertakings, entailing years of work, could not be kept secret. The spoil was too rich and tempting. Grave robbers set about their stealthy business.

For generations stonemasons, painters, artists of every kind, labourers and captives turned the sun seared cliffs into a honeycomb of graves. Garrisons of mercenaries lived constantly on the site to protect the royal burial places. Nevertheless, spoliation increased to such an extent that the priests and nobles were distraught. So began the frantic moving of royal corpses from tomb to tomb. Treasures and jewels vanished but the faithful did their best to hide and protect the royal mummies from outrage.

Eventually some 40 sarcophagi with the mortal remains of a galaxy of such mighty Pharaohs as Ramses II and Thothmes III, were placed together in a 35 foot deep shaft which penetrated into the cliff face near Deir-el-Bahri. Here they remained in peace for over 3000 years until, by the merest chance, the shaft was discovered in 1875.

It is with a mixture of awe and curiosity that tourists sail across the Nile to visit the Valley of the Kings and see some of these remarkable tombs for themselves. It is impossible to view many in one day, although there are over 40 open to the public. Mollie Emery, wife of Bryan Emery was most amused to overhear a remark by one lady tourist to another when they left their hotel. 'You do the tombs dear, and I'll do the Temples!'

The vast tombs hewn in the Valley of the Kings were made between 1050 and 1700 B.C. You step ashore where, in the days of Thebes, a great avenue of jackal-sphinxes swept back from the quayside and led to Amenophis III's mortuary temple. It is astonishing to find fleets of taxis at places like this.

Once beyond the village and narrow strip of river cultivation, you drive into a rocky valley boasting not a single blade of grass. Fierce sunlight beats downward between the hills as if in a furnace, flaring into every crevice. The road winds and twists as you go up between bare cliffs. Against the periwinkle blue of the sky scarified hilltops are dazzlingly bright. So glittering white are the peaks that they might be snowcapped. The Theban hills are as relentless as the death they cover. Down beneath them, burrowed into their very heart, is hidden the splendour of ancient Egypt.

Each grave is numbered and each has electric light. Suitable steps and gangplanks enable you to descend with ease and safety to see the unforgettable paintings in the depths beneath. Space does not enable me to describe many. But you must not miss tomb 240, final resting place of King Tutankhamen.

There is little decoration on the walls and you soon reach the main chamber. It is well proportioned though not large. Beyond the deep well where the sarcophagus rests, the wall is painted with life-like figures. A high priest, clad in a symbolic tiger skin, is presenting offerings to the God Osiris. The tiger skin appears so real that if it was touched its tawny surface must surely feel like fur. Next to the God stands Pharaoh Tutankhamen, his wife (so beautiful it is obvious she was the daughter of the famed Queen Nefertiti) and their two children. The royal physician stands beside the diminutive princesses. All are robed in the finest white linen.

On the left wall are 12 squares depicting the 12 months of the year. Symbolic murals cover the right wall in the centre of which is the sacred boat of Amen Ra. Above it is the goddess of the Soul shown in the form of a bird, wings spread out protectively, with the Key of Life clasped in its claws.

You lean over the wooden railings to look down at the sarcophagus whose cover has been replaced with glass through which can be seen a golden replica of the young King. Here rested the body of Tutankhamen, living image of Amen, who ruled an empire that stretched from the fourth cataract to the Nile Delta. His golden mask radiates the same beneficent tranquil expression as the golden replicas in the Cairo Museum. All the gold furniture in the Tutankhamen Gallery was discovered in this vault by Dr Howard Carter in 1922.

Tomb number 9 was wrought into the cliffs in 1200 B.C. for Ramses VI. When it was first violated is not known. The tomb had been much visited during the Greek-Roman period as can be seen by signatures on some of the walls. From these inscriptions it is learned that at that time, the tomb was wrongfully supposed to be Memnon's. There was no body to prove otherwise. When the priests of Amen discovered the tomb had been plundered they had removed the royal mummy and rehidden it in the tomb of Amenhotep II. From the days of the Roman Empire the empty tomb was forgotten. Some 57 years ago a wealthy villager who was interested in archaeology rediscovered its entrance.

Ramses VI was an elderly man when he died and work on his vault had continued for many years. On the day of his death the artists and craftsmen working on the site put down the tools of their trade as was customary. The old King, with abundant food to start his long journey through the underworld, was laid reverently in the royal sarcophagus and buried among his rich funerary furnishings. At his demise members of his entourage were put to death and entombed with him.

You can see the Tuat dangers that confronted the Pharaoh – green and yellow twisting serpents and evil looking crocodiles. There is the Pharaoh in the act of presenting offerings to the various gods. The king's wealth can be judged by the paintings of the many chariots, furnishings, animals, numerous jars of wine, oil and perfumes.

Down, down you go into the subterranean vault, down through cool passages of beautiful paintings, hieroglyphics and cartouches. At the end of each shaft-like corridor you come to a bend that, with the aid of large mirrors, had reflected the sun further down into the next stone corridor so that artists could have light to paint by.

In this house of death the walls are covered with scenes of life; pictures of slaves and prisoners who took part in the building of this place. Some, near the site of the sarcophagus, are headless, their shame pictured on the walls so that other prisoners could take warning of what happened should a man pause, however briefly, in his pursuit of duty for the Pharaoh. Many artists are shown painting upside down, hanging from their heads in places they could not reach by standing. Thus they retained the right perspective and their arms hung free to paint walls with a steady brush.

When it is remembered what fabulous things were discovered in Tutankhamen's small tomb the imagination fails to conjure up what fantastic wealth Ramses VI's burial vault yielded.

In 1899 a wall of living stone beyond a deep sunken well in the mountain face was tested by the French archaeologist Victor Loret. It sounded hollow. Excavations were begun and Tomb 35, that of Amenhotep II was discovered. The deeply dug shaft had served to put would-be marauders off the trail for hundreds of years. It was a most exciting find, for not only was much treasure uncovered but several royal mummies were found with the mummy of Pharaoh Amenhotep II – the bodies of Ramses IV, Ramses V, Ramses VI, Thothmes IV, Amenophis III and Menephthah. The burial vault had obviously been used as a royal hiding place by priests for Pharaohs whose tombs had been molested. Many of these mummies are now in the Cairo Museum.

The excavations were so meticulously carried out that none of the painted walls or columns has suffered in any way. It is as though the colours had been applied yesterday. Painted stars shine down through a bright stone ceiling. Dressed in transparent fine linen, comely life-size figures on high square pillars are illuminated in one hall. Strip lighting is embedded in the framework of elongated glass windows which cover and protect the paintings. Many are of the Gods Hathor and Anubis, giving the Key of Life to members of the Royal Family.

The colourful figures of these royal men and women appear to be alive so that the hall seems peopled with nobles and ladies from long ago. It is fascinating to see that both men and women had enamelled their finger and toe nails white!

Tomb 17, that of Seti 1, was discovered by Belzoni. It is the deepest burial vault in the world. Two downward flights of steps lead into a long inclined passage way which is joined to chambers and halls by narrow stairways. The walls are covered with religious scenes depicting the journey of Seti accompanied by Amen Ra, through the Tuat. The length of this house of death reaches some 500 feet and the depth is about 150 feet.

As usual the day the Pharaoh died work ceased and Seti I's personal architect and many of his entourage were put to death and entombed with him. This ensured that no one lived, save the priests, who knew the way to the subterranean passages of the secret, treasure-filled burial vault.

Two pillared halls and antechambers lead to the final resting place of the sarcophagus. The high vaulting overhead is supported by six pillars cut from the rock. The walls are smooth to the touch and covered with coloured paintings. The colours are most vivid. The ceiling, with authentic starry constellations, is of midnight blue save in the space exactly over the sarcophagus where there is a carved circular zodiac. The river of the Tuat flows along one wall. Breaking the surface is a fat-bellied crocodile, its wide jaws open, drops of water sliding off its green scales. The Goddess Isis reclines gracefully in a sacred barge. A gigantic scarab clings to the flat surface of the wall, ebony black in colour.

The sarcophagus has gone. Belzoni offered it for sale and eventually it was sold for £2,000 to Sir John Soane. It is one of the most beautiful of its kind and is now in the Soane Museum in Lincoln's Inn Fields, London. Made from the finest alabaster it is inscribed with scenes and texts of the 'Book of Gates'. It is sculptured inside and out with hundreds of delicately carved figures, each about two inches in height. The niche where the sarcophagus once rested seems very small in the stately hall of the burial vault.

Divided from the Valley of the Kings by a high ridge of cliffs lies Deir-el-Bahri, the magnificent temple of Queen Hatshepsut, one of the mightiest, wealthiest queens of all time. Her family tree is so inter-related it has proved a headache for genealogists ever since she died. She was daughter of Thothmes I and the latter's half sister Aahmes. Her father's second wife, Mut-Nefert, bore a son who became Thothmes II. He married his half sister Hatshepsut. Thothmes II married a second wife – a woman of low rank who bore him an heir. So it came about that Hatshepsut was a half sister and wife of Thothmes II and was made guardian of her stepson and nephew who became Thothmes III.

Dearly beloved by her father and ambitious to a degree, Hatshepsut even before the age of 16, held great sway in her father's kingdom. Her power increased greatly after her father died and Thothmes II came to the throne; so much so that gradually most of the state administration came under her direct jurisdiction. Thothmes II, a born warrior, was delighted. He had no interest whatever in the perplexed intricacies of court life and spent most of his time away from Thebes fighting rewarding battles in Nubia, and warring against the raiding tribes of the Eastern Desert. Probably due to the hard life imposed by these numerous campaigns he died while still a young man.

To retain the throne that had been virtually hers, Hatshepsut went through a form of marriage with her nephew Thothmes III.

Incestuous as all this sounds, it was the practice in those days to keep the royal blood pure by family intermarriage, thus assuring that the actual blood running in the veins of the Pharaohs remained divine and unsullied – a semi mystic belief to preserve the god-relationship.

Thothmes III being but a child when his father died, the ambitious Hatshepsut soon cast her role of co-regent aside, and, donning the King's attire literally, with all the insignia of royalty (including the ritual false beard) she assumed full Pharaonic status.

The young prince disliked Hatshepsut and hated court life as heartily as his father before him. As he grew he dreamed of going far from Hatshepsut's dictatorial sway and becoming a great warrior like Thothmes II. On reaching manhood he begged leave of the Queen to prove himself on the fields of battle. Hatshepsut would not give her consent, realising full well if anything should happen to the young man her power would weaken. So Thothmes III remained in Thebes and led the life expected of a prince. He offered sacrifices to the Gods, was carried in processions, took part in ceremonies and for 22 years was dominated by Hatshepsut.

Thothmes' dislike of the Queen grew into hatred as he became older and, although at her command he had married her daughter, when the great Hatshepsut died he took his revenge. He ordered all her portraits to be erased, her statues and obelisks broken and he would have damaged all her memorials had he not suddenly realised he was at last free to do as he wished. The long years of self-discipline and ambition were unleashed, and into the pages of history marched Thothmes the Great – one of the most famous warrior Pharaohs of dynastic times.

The powerful sway Queen Hatshepsut held over her people during her lifetime can be glimpsed at Deir-el-Bahri where her glorification reached its zenith. Her royal architect Senmut, a notable man of the calibre of Amenophis, one of the most distinguished architects ever, created this unique temple for the sole purpose that offerings might be made there throughout the ages to the Queen's Ka on festival days.

The temple, one of the most beautiful in Egypt, consists of three pillared terraces in the style we now call Grecian, yet it preceded such buildings in Greece by a thousand years. It is built into a bronze semi-circular backdrop of barren mountain which has an unbroken summit of some 400 feet. Its fissured walls, born of centuries of wind and scorching sun, swell outward in cloud-shaped curves with the odd proportions of a Dali painting. Although at a distance the slender columns appear to support the sheer upright mountain behind it, the illusion does not detract from the temple's elegant beauty.

At midday the monument seems to recapture the glory of the past. The sun beats on the pillars so that they gleam like old ivory. Behind the temple the bare stone of the mountainside shines like copper. Over all hangs the vivid blue canopy of the sky.

At Deir-el-Bahri there is not the usual temple entrance through an H-shaped pylon. Immense porticoes, with square columns, lead off the processional ramp at different levels. At the top the visitor finds the Holy of Holies, a shrine built into the mountainside. The open colonnaded courts have variously designed pillars, many of them 16 sided.

Long ago the great portals were of wrought bronze and embellished with figures in metal work. The terraces were ornamented with trees, flowers and beds of papyrus. The temple was approached by an avenue of sphinxes 500 yards long.

While standing on the wide entablature and looking back towards the Nile one can see a magnificent view down the sloping rocky valley, which stretches into the far distance in a blue shimmering heat haze.

The temple's colonnades lead into great halls and chambers. The atmosphere is still permeated with the glamour and splendour of Hatshepsut. Her presence is felt throughout Deir-el-Bahri and your first glimpse of her is as a sculptured figure on a wall. She stands, every inch a queen, beautiful, slender and mysterious, beneath a ceiling of midnight blue studded with red stars. Her subjects are presenting offerings at her feet from great mounds of incense. Squadrons of her soldiers march protectively in the background.

There is a lovely painting of the sacred cow of Hathor in burnt siena colouring. A number of pictures seek to prove that the procreation and birth of Hatshepsut was divine. Amen himself is seen talking to the Queen Mother Aahmes, confiding that: 'Hatshepsut shall be the name of thy daughter (yet to be born) . . . she shall exercise the excellent Kingship in this whole land.' Gods are pictured bringing their offerings at the birth of the daughter of Amen.

In one hall there are undamaged carvings of maidens and youths bearing offerings for sacrifice. One figure carries a spray of lotus blossom, one a platter of fruit, another a goblet of wine. A young man drags a reluctant bull calf beside a boy who leads a small gazelle. These figures are about one fifth life size, their colouring fresh and the features expressive.

The most beautifully carved murals are in a horizontal broad band of sculpture at eye level along one wall. Each tiny detail is exquisitely modelled. There is no feeling of flatness although the small figures are never raised more than one third of an inch above the background. The frieze tells a story of high adventure.

Hatshepsut was commanded by the divine oracle to procure myrrh trees to be planted in the terraces of Deir-el-Bahri. Myrrh trees were unknown throughout the length and breadth of Egypt. Nothing daunted, the Queen, determined that the command be fulfilled, dispatched a convoy of vessels to the land of Punt to obtain the trees by the peaceful method of barter.

The ships sailed to the west coast of Africa, up the Elephant River near Cape Guardafui and moored near one of the inland native villages. Merchandise had been carried, including a large statue of the Queen herself, to use in exchange for the trees.

Unfortunately, the carving showing this was stolen but it has been replaced by a substitute and there are drawings of the original in many archaeologists' books. In it the Prince of Punt was shown accompanied by his family. His wife wore a yellow transparent robe and was most unusually fat. As on temple walls royal figures are invariably slender many Egyptologists believe that the Princess of Punt suffered from elephantiasis.

The rest of the picture story is complete. The natives give great quantities of gold as well as other lavish presents to Hatshepsut so that they greatly exceed those sent from Egypt. Amongst them is a rare southern panther, especially caught for Her Majesty, together with leopards, monkeys and baboons. There are spices, aromatic woods, incense, eye cosmetics, ebony, cinnamon-wood, tropical plants and the myrrh trees.

The frescoes of life in Punt are enchanting. Hutments can be seen with various domestic animals in the foreground. A pastoral scene shows three cows lingering to browse whilst the rest of the herd move slowly under the shade of heavily branched trees. The Queen's ship lies alongside being loaded for the long journey home. The cordage, made from palm fibre, appears to be like the rigging of today.

You can see the famous myrrh trees being carried aboard,

each planted in a great urn to enable it to survive the voyage, each slung by ropes on the shoulders of six men. The ships are deep in the water because of the heavily piled gifts. Myrrh trees are stacked fore and aft. Baboons play on top of the cargo, more gifts are to come. Men stride up the gangplanks, their backs bent under the weight of sacks.

Most fascinating of all is the artistic licence with which the sea creatures are drawn beneath the water. Easily discerned are giant rays, sharks, swordfish and whales.

The ships return to Egypt with rich cargo and the adventurous undertaking ends happily. The myrrh trees are set in the gardens of the temple. The oracle is content and Hatshepsut is well pleased.

During Hatshepsut's reign Egyptian trade flourished and temple building reached artistic proportions not known before. Due to her beauty, foresight and iron will, she sought to prove to her subjects that to a queen and a goddess in particular, nothing is impossible.

For centuries travellers have come to ancient Thebes, the Valley of the Kings and the Valley of the Queens to gaze and marvel. Achilles described it to Odysseus as a place where 'through every one of a hundred gates two hundred warriors with their chariots and horses come.' Diodorus told of its great wealth and temples. Where else can such an impressive array of ruins be seen? It is impossible to cover all of it even in several visits. The tombs of the nobles are as fascinating in their way as those of the great kings. Each temple is different and, in the early morning, perhaps nothing is more impressive than to drive along the great spaces that stretch to the Colossi of Memnon.

As has been mentioned before the air is so crystal clear in Egypt that one's sense of distance is upset. It is only when you leave your car and walk towards the two mammoth figures of the Colossi that you notice small black dots moving at their feet. These prove to be other tourists. Gargantuan and impassive the statues sit brooding over flat plainland, survivors of 3000 years.

The Colossi face the rising sun and at their gigantic feet the rural life of Egypt follows cycle on cycle. Fellaheen plough the land, the crops grow and are gathered in. Second in size only to the Sphinx they tower a good 60 feet above the ground. The mighty shoulders are 20 feet across, the forearms from elbow to finger tip 15 feet and the fingers are over four feet long.

Mystery veils the Colossi. Originally each was carved from one huge piece of stone and they were placed before the funerary temple of Amenophis III, a building which has long since disappeared. The cartouche of this Pharaoh, of whom there are replicas, can still be seen inscribed on their backs.

Sightseers come and stare in silence, then walk thoughtfully back to waiting cars. Not so travellers of an earlier age, for where the legs and feet are not already covered with hieratic writing they are engraved with Latin and Greek signatures. Hadrian, during a three day visit with his consort had his royal poet inscribe on one Colossus a poem which can still be seen. One verse implies that the Emperor was greeted by one of the Memnon singing three different notes.

Some 1,400 years after the Colossi had been erected it was rumoured that they represented the Trojan hero Memnon and that the Northern Colossus emitted musical notes when the sun rose each morning. According to Petronianus it made a sighing utterance to its mother, Eros the Dawn, because of injuries imposed upon it by Cambyses. Be this as it may, other Roman visitors beside the Emperor Hadrian heard the 'vocal Memnon'. As one Colossus was fractured the sound may have been caused when the wind blew in a certain direction. Some historians claim it was a priest intoning. When Septimus Severus had the damaged Colossus restored there was no more mention of this phenomenon.

These mammoth figures become almost human at sunset when they are backlit. They sit, hands on knees, upright in their massive chairs, gaining in grandeur as dusk shrouds them and the western cliffs of Thebes still brood over many of the splendours of the old necropolis, not least among them the mortuary temple of Ramses II – the Ramesseum.

Ramses II was by far the most prolific of all the royal builders and the Ramesseum was his greatest achievement. It is reminiscent of Karnak, although the latter was completed over 15 centuries and under the reign of a dozen kings, whereas the Ramesseum was created during Ramses II's lifetime.

Ramses knew full well Karnak could not be equalled in size during a few years but he kept its magnificent example in mind and sought to equal its majesty. He knew speed resulted in careless work. This did not worry him when having his accomplishments recorded in the temples of previous Pharaohs but for the Ramesseum, built for his glory alone, nothing but the best was good enough. It was to make up in beauty what it lacked in size.

The roof was supported along the length of the hypostyle hall by eight rows of beautiful columns, resembling but smaller than, those at Karnak. Lotus-bud pillars were dwarfed by central aisle columns 36 feet in height and culminating in outward-flowing lotus flowers.

Only part of the roofing remains. One can stand beneath it looking up and drink in the beauty of the tapering pillars, unfolding their lotus petals so gracefully that they appear to cling to, rather than support the roof.

It is heartbreaking that so much of this splendid building was pulled down by vandals. Yet majesty rises from wreckage like the statues of Ramses II which remain standing in front of most of the surviving pillars. Ramses II tells of his great victory at Kadesh in the temples of Luxor, Karnak, Abydos and Abu Simbel, but nowhere do the reliefs portray the battle in a more lively manner than at The Ramesseum.

The history of this famous battle began in 1288 B.C. when Ramses led his divisions across Palestine to the Lebanon. Fighting between the Egyptians and the Hittites had continued for many years and the Pharaoh determined that his army should defeat the Hittites once and for all. He was confident of success and this feeling grew as he bypassed towns which he had laid waste in previous campaigns.

One rosy dawn, impatient to get to grips with the enemy, Ramses, together with his household troops and leaving the bulk of his army to follow later, forded the Orontes. His spies had found no trace of the enemy and two roving Beduin had told of the Hittite King's flight to the north. With joy in his heart the young Pharaoh pressed on to Kadesh.

The Hittite king, Metella, had been cunning. The two roving Beduin had been well paid to tell their story. In reality the King knew each move the Pharaoh made and bided his time. As the small Egyptian cavalcade rode forward their enemies stealthily followed.

Later in the day Ramses and his retinue made preparations to bivouac near the Orontes river. Two Asiatic prisoners were dragged before the Pharaoh. They brought bad news. The small Egyptian encampment was surrounded. Before Ramses could take in these dire tidings the Hittites closed in.

Without hesitation the Pharaoh mounted his war chariot and, with his pet lion loping beside it and a faithful few around him, threw himself on the enemy at the edge of the river. At one time he was left alone but continued to fight with fury casting his enemies one after another into the Orontes.

Of all the lively reliefs of the battle of Kadesh none draws a smile more than one showing the Chief of Aleppo held upside down by his men to disgorge water after having been dragged from the river. On the opposite side of the narrow river King Metella was astonished to see his own royal brother and personal scribe go down with many others before the fury of the young Pharaoh, but Fate was kind to Ramses. Before his brave onslaught at the riverside was over, the main body of his army arrived and converged on the Hittites, who, already plundering the Pharaoh's bivouac, were in turn caught by surprise. Heartened by the timely arrival of his soldiers, Pharaoh rallied his forces and the battle raged for three more hours. As sunset coloured the fallen standards of the Hittites the Egyptians carried the day.

Some 15 years later peace was finally signed between the Egyptians and the Hittites and, in 1259 B.C., Ramses married Metella's eldest daughter, so consolidating the peaceful intentions of both countries forever. Ramses bestowed the name Matnefrure on the Hittite Princess meaning, 'Who sees the beauty of Ra.'

Ramses' battle prowess spread far and wide through the Asiatic lands and it was a common belief that he was a suckling of their warlike goddess Anat. Pleased with this reputation Ramses renamed his favourite daughter Daughter of Anat.

As Thothmes III followed the example of Thothmes II, so Ramses III imitated the ways of Ramses II. He rode to war with his pet lion bounding beside his chariot, called his children by the same names, and determined to have his own mortuary temple built during his lifetime.

When Thebes first became the capital of Egypt it was believed that one of the primordial hills of the earth was situated within the precincts of what later became the temple district of Medinet Habu. It was here that Ramses III decided his funerary temple should be built.

The project was attacked with all the vigour to be expected of a man of action, son of a great warrior. Architects, artists, craftsmen of all kinds, voluntary immigrants, prisoners and forced labour commenced work under the royal command. There are signs of carelessness due to extreme haste, but Ramses III lived to see the day when the temple of his dreams became a reality.

Gone is the exquisite sculpture of his grandfather Seti I, the fine workmanship of Ramses II. Instead there is the massive grandeur of a warrior King to whom, it was said, the gods were shields in time of battle, hovering around the royal war chariot. The architecture is heavy, ponderous and lasting.

Two vast courts are fronted by gigantic pylons and enriched with bud columns. Thick square piers back vigorous statues of the King. The hypostyle hall is narrow, flanked on either side by small chambers and leads into three less grandiose pillared halls through a maze of passages and antechambers. Two of the latter have waist high shelves all around them and were used as Offering Rooms, one for fruit and food, the other for flowers, perfumes and wine.

No corner of the interior is left without murals. Ramses is shown presenting offerings to the God of Fertility. In a relief on the back of the first pylon the King can be seen hunting

22. *The Sphinx at Giza*
23. *The Alabaster Sphinx at Memphis*

wild bulls. A whole wall shows the Pharaoh being borne on a silken-hung litter in a festival procession. It is led by two lines of priests carrying banners and golden furniture from the temple. Precedence is given to a snowy white bull, sacred to the god Min, in whose honour the festival must have been held. The Queen is with the Pharaoh and the royal couple are surrounded by courtiers, fan bearers and priests carrying censers. A singer entertains the procession.

Scene follows scene like a play so that you can enter a life lived thousands of years ago. One wall shows the King judging his enemies. From his golden chariot he metes out justice to those who dared turn a hand against him. Hordes of prisoners are before him. They are to be castrated and have their right hands hacked off. The sentence fills the captives with terror and Pharaoh magnanimously commands that they shall be fed before their ordeal. Great mounds of mutilated pieces are proof that the sentences were carried out. Yet hundreds of prisoners of war survived their mutilation and helped to build this very temple.

On the inward slope of one of the pylons it is inscribed that Ramses III reigned for 31 years. His victories were many but, like so many great warriors, there was more than a streak of cruelty in his god-like character. Watching the Pharaoh club his enemies to death in one carving are captives from Phoenicia, Cyprus, Syria and other parts of Africa, the names of their countries inscribed on their bodies. Although merely symbolic it is a cruel picture.

Other reliefs denoting strength are of a less horrific nature: the Pharaoh lion hunting, a naval battle, beautifully carved. It is unique – the first naval battle to be recorded in history. The King is seen shooting at the hostile fleet from the land. One humane touch is depicted: Egyptian soldiers are swimming to rescue drowning sailors. Finally, as with kings since time began, the Pharaoh is shown on the balcony of his palace receiving ovations from his subjects.

So deep are the hieroglyphic incisions that one day, in this temple, I put my right hand into the curve of a cartouche. Even with my fingers straight my hand sank into the wall up

24. A Nubian 'fellah'

to the wrist. Obviously Ramses III was determined that no one should obliterate his royal signatures and writings as had been done to Pharaohs before him.

In every way this temple differs from the Ramesseum. Though open to the sky in many places, Medinet Habu is enclosed within itself, broodingly secret and quiet. The deeper wall incisions with their sombre black depths emphasise a feeling of sadness despite the victorious battle scenes. Even the small figures of Ramses' Queen behind the Pharaoh's leg like those at Karnak, fail to lighten the atmosphere. Perhaps it is because Ramses III was the last of a line of heroic kings – the last great sovereign of ancient Egypt. However, the real delight of Medinet Habu is the galaxy of colour still remaining on walls thousands of years old.

Two coloured ceilings are wondrously preserved, where the cool blue-green of turquoise predominates. An amusing plump water bird struts along one segment of ceiling, its feathers red, blue and white, its beak a shiny hydrangea blue!

When I first went to the Valley of the Kings the roads were bumpy and there were no rest houses. Today there are buses and taxis on macadam roads, electricity has been installed and eventually all the temples will be floodlit at night.

9 The Temples at Kom Ombo, Edfu, Esnah, Denderah and Abydos

For centuries the most enjoyable way to see the ancient temples of Upper Egypt has been by Nile boat visiting each place in turn. The Pharaohs started the delightful habit thousands of years ago and it has continued ever since. The sunny days pass pleasantly always ending with technicolour sunsets reflected in the shining water. At dusk birds wing their way across the river to the banks and sheltering trees. Flocks of snowy egrets settle together in trees which, in the half light and far away, appear to be weighed down with giant magnolia blooms. You go ashore sight seeing for much of the day but return for meals to your restful floating hotel. There is no packing of suitcases or the trouble of moving from place to place each day.

I have done the trip from Aswan to Cairo but the reverse is also offered by such firms as Swans Educational, Bales and Cooks. The latter are building two new ships of their own. The other leg of the journey to join or leave the ship is by rail or air. The last time I was in Egypt all the cruises were fully booked and I visited the various temples by car. This has its advantages in that the roads are very good, the scenery varied and you can dovetail the visits in to suit your own particular schedule. However it is not at the moment very practical to drive the whole 600 miles from Cairo. The road signs are in Arabic and there is not as yet any self-drive car hire organisation.

Each visitor will form his own ideas about the merits of the various temples and the order in which to visit them but it is difficult to ensure that you keep the best until last. For my own part none of them equals Edfu. The simplicity and dignity of its vaulted halls with their air of tranquillity, the slender columns and the last final glimpse of its bronze coloured pylon as one drives away, leave me with a feeling of serenity that I have not met elsewhere.

If time is short you can do a half day tour by taxi from Aswan to the temple at Kom Ombo and if you leave just after breakfast you can carry on to Edfu and still return to Aswan for a late lunch. Kom Ombo is some 40 kilometres distant and you drive along an asphalt road close to the Nile which comes into view now and then. You take another road which branches off to the left opposite the village of Shoteb and almost immediately you can see part of the pylon of Kom Ombo temple perched high above the surrounding countryside on a plateau overlooking the Nile.

The morning I went with some friends several tourists were already mounting the 25 steps which lead to the entrance. Just inside the gateway was the statue of an elderly Roman in a toga. Open sandals disclosed wrinkled feet. His thin frame was in sharp contrast to the youthful and well-formed bodies usually portrayed on temple walls. Pharaohs are always shown as young, virile men. A few steps from the statue there was a sort of tomb or shrine open at one end to the air. 'Here is something which was of great interest hundreds of years before Roman times,' said a guide gesturing towards it. As we got closer we could see that its front wall was damaged and it was reinforced with bars so that it had a cell-like appearance. The guide stood back so that we might look inside. In semi-darkness, pierced by filtered light, we could see what appeared to be somnolent crocodiles.

'Are they alive?' shuddered one lady.

'No Madam,' answered the guide.

'If they are not alive how do they keep in this hot climate?' persisted the lady.

'Are they mummified?' asked one of the tourists quietly.

'Yes,' nodded the guide 'they are the actual Holy Crocodiles of Kom Ombo'.

We looked at the mummies. Their white teeth were bared

their scales were black and dusty. It was incomprehensible that such cultivated people as the ancient Egyptians could worship such abhorrent creatures. Yet it was so.

When these reptiles were alive ear rings of gold hung from their saurian ears. Stunted forepaws had been encircled with jewelled bracelets. From Hieratic writing it is learned that dignified priests decked the horny overlapping scales with gems and gently pushed rich food into snapping jaws.

A few minutes later, walking away from the mummies, we saw a small stone lioness about three feet high, as beautiful as the crocodiles were ugly. It sat like a cat, front legs neatly placed between its back ones. Its scrolled fur was thick and curly over its curved back.

We walked towards the temple and in a few minutes we were staring down into the monstrous darkness of a deep Nilometer. It was in the usual form of a well, but was far larger and deeper than the one on Elephantine Island. Its depth could be judged from different levels by descending a circular stone staircase.

Wishing to see the temple from a vantage point at the far end of the courtyard, I carefully picked my way over crumbling masonry and came upon a beautiful relief on a great chunk of the north wall. It was of Ptolemy IX, and showed the King fowling from a boat on the marshes of the Nile. A cloud of pintails, each feather as perfectly reproduced as if in a photograph, fanned out and fluttered up into the stone sky from a profusion of slender reeds and lotus blossoms.

The temple which had been excavated in 1883, had high lotus topped columns and was mostly open to the sky. It towered into the blue from its well-trodden stone base. Worship here had been divided between two gods, Herun (another form of Horus) and Sebek, the Holy Crocodile. Traces of colourful Pharaonic designs could be seen on the cornice and the inside roofing.

Reliefs carved on the walls long ago told of deeds and wonders and could still be read today as easily as a book. Signs of the fruitfulness of the Nile appeared again and again in the form of a figure pouring water from an urn which flowed into bread, grapes and flowers. A physician could be seen in his surgery. His instruments were displayed for us – scissors, scales, spoons, vials of medicine, and herbs. Two patients were waiting to see him, one a woman heavy with child. Captives were shown tied upside down to the prows of ships returning home after a successful campaign.

Roman influence is very evident at Kom Ombo, the summits of the columns were of Roman design and beyond the temple stood the remains of Roman pillars. These once continued in an avenue to the great door of the temple, which was made of heavy sycamore wood.

The last we saw of Kom Ombo as we walked back to our cars were the remains of Roman houses clustered around the outer walls of the temple.

We rejoined the Aswan Road and carried on towards Edfu. After passing a Nubian village the road snaked for some kilometres between eroded desert hills interspersed now and then with tilled fields and palm groves. Villages came and went and finally the Nile reappeared and we crossed a bridge to the west bank where we entered Edfu. It is an expanding little place but its fame rests on the magnificent temple of Horus, the most complete monument in Egypt of its date. It stands alone, well away from the town.

Close by the temple we came upon the Andrea Rest House. Little tables with wicker chairs were spread with gay tablecloths beneath shady trees and it was pleasant to rest and drink iced beer before visiting the temple.

It is difficult when seeing Edfu temple in its marvellous state of preservation to remember that it was blanketed by dry desert for centuries. Only 80 years ago parts of it lay beneath a village and visitors had to clamber down a sheer hill to get inside.

It was begun by Ptolemy III but maintains the traditions of Ramses' period a thousand years before. It took 180 years to build and its relief work nearly a century to complete. It was finished, just as it stands today, 57 years before the birth of Christ. Its magnificently proportioned stone structure, almost apricot in colour, is a living testimony to the refined taste of

Ptolemaic rulers who were great patrons of literature and the arts. Splendid towers soar 112 feet into the air. Resplendent with cartouches, hieroglyphics and pictures, the walls stretch for more than 400 feet.

We entered an open courtyard where, supported by 32 pillars, there was a three-sided gallery. At the gateway we paused to look at a small sphinx.

Within the court stood two large stone figures of Horus, one on either side of the entrance to the temple. Very different indeed were these magnificent statues, with their mighty folded wings, compared to the mummified crocodiles at Kom Ombo.

The architect had created six beautiful halls. As one leads into the next the impression is given of rising roofs and lowering floor levels. The spirit grows as the body shrinks. Each hall used to open into the next through a sycamore door of which only the hinge recesses remain. When at last the sanctuary of Horus himself is reached, one can imagine the soft footsteps of priests and the god's wings hovering protectively overhead. High above us the vaulting was black with the smoke from many sacrifices. A small black granite altar lay before the shrine wherein the statue of Horus had been placed. The bust of the god was a crowned hawk head of pure gold which is now in the Cairo Museum. The god's eyes gaze fixedly into space and around his golden neck hangs a blue scarab.

Ten chambers surround the sanctuary but are so dark that candles or torches have to be used to enable the drawings on the walls to be seen. In one Isis and Osiris are embracing, while in another there are sacred baboons, symbols of learning. On yet another wall a handsome Pharaoh is seen presenting a vase of wine to Horus, while near him the figure of a priest is offering incense. All the delightful well-known Pharaonic signs are here, the Key of Life, the Staff of Happiness and the Lotus, divine symbol of resurrection.

Unfortunately many of the faces of the gods and Pharaohs are partially obliterated. Christians caused much damage of this kind in the temples along the Nile during the early

Christian era.

Blinking as we came out into the sunlit courtyard from the darkness of the temple we went to see the inevitable Nilometer, so essential in the days of Pharaonic Egypt.

We examined the outer walls of the courtyard and followed the reliefs around the three sides of a square. They show a Pharaoh fighting his enemies, harpooning a hippopotamus, riding a lion and other vigorous pursuits as well as more peaceful facets of the King's life.

I joined some of the other tourists climbing up inside one of the towers. As it was dark, guides led the way carrying lanterns. Up and up we went, around and around. Ten steps would lead to a flat circular piece of stonework, six steps would lead to the next piece of flooring, ten steps again, more flooring, six steps, more flooring, and so this was repeated until we had climbed 252 steps and came out into the vivid sunshine at the top.

The perfect symmetry of the temple lay beneath us. The little town of Edfu stretched to the right, rolling green fields to the left. Straight ahead glittered the Nile, while far away on the horizon, the gold of the desert melted into the blue sky.

Cheek by jowl with Edfu railway station there is an excellent restaurant called 'Andrea' owned by a man of that name who also owns the Andrea Resthouse already mentioned. Andrea Vourganas and his wife, Mary, who speaks five languages including English, run the restaurant together with a willing staff. It is surprisingly large for such an out-of-the-way place. The menu is a long one and the food delicious. Suffice to quote a few comments from their Golden Book: 'On a spur of the moment excursion from Luxor to Edfu we were taken in hand by Andrea and his wife, given a splendid meal and sent on our way rejoicing.' signed by a professor from Toronto University. A member of the American Embassy staff from Cairo has written: 'Egypt's best restaurant. Thanks for delicious and very pleasant meal.' A member of the British Embassy wrote: 'Had a marvellous stay in Edfu. Temple is the most interesting one in Egypt. I highly recommend Mr and Mrs Andrea for their hospitality, friendly atmosphere and delicious meal.' But perhaps the comments which pleased Andrea and Mary most were signed by Prince and Princess Mikasa, brother and sister in law of the Japanese Emperor in February 1975, 'Enjoyed very much the time with you visiting the marvellous, complete, wonderful masterpiece Horus Temple. We shall not forget your hearty welcome and your delicious meal which we enjoyed so much and we shall recommend it to our friends and guests everywhere. Congratulations to you both for the wonderful meal and excellent service.'

The temples of Esnah, Denderah and Abydos are most easily reached by car from Luxor. Indeed you can reach Esnah in under the hour. The temple is dedicated to the ram-headed god Khnum and, as it is in the centre of the little town, it is best to park your car or taxi a short distance away. I shared a car with some other tourists early one morning to do this and we set off with a guide leading the way and walked along a narrow road which had been newly watered to keep the dust down. Merchants were plying their trades from the frontless shops. Two women passed us shrouded in check blankets of white and black, youths were making an orange eiderdown on some freshly scrubbed pavement. The pungent smell of new wood shavings betrayed the carpenter, whose workshop overflowed onto the pavement. A small boy was busily sanding down the front of a drawer which would soon join its fellows in a tall chest. The minute particles hung in the sunny air. An old man was selling fascinating dolls made of sequins and beads. Another merchant offered us colourfully woven baskets. The town is really famous for its lentils, one of the staple foods of the country folk.

We approached a high, long railing and looking over it saw a deep excavation below. At the far end of it was the temple of Khnum, the powerful deity who, with his potter's wheel, had brought many other gods to life. Khnum wears the Atef crown, the crescent moon and disc, and his wife, the Goddess of the Countryside, a girdle of lotus blossom. She holds a plantation covered with wild fowl in her hands and the hieratic sign for a field on her head.

Thothmes III founded a temple on this same site long ago but the monument we were now looking at was of a far later date and bore the name of several Roman emperors. As at Edfu, a complete village had been built over it. When a house was demolished some 70 years ago, instead of the usual mud foundations, stone roofing was found and from this began the uncovering of the temple.

A man unlocked a gateway in the railings and courteously bowed us through to a staircase which led to the temple below. As we went down we could look at the temple from various levels. The cornice retained colouring and was heavily sculptured. We walked across the excavation and went in through the temple portico. Twenty-four columns, deeply engraved with pictures, surrounded the large hall we entered. On the right wall was a fresco of the Emperor Claudius being carried in procession. The Emperor was the same Claudius who first had the Bible translated into Greek.

During the Christian era two chambers had been built into the facade of the building near where we stood, one as a library, the other to be used by priests as a vestry.

A zodiac could just be discerned in the soot from a thousand sacrifices in the ceiling above. In sharp contrast bright reds, yellows and blues remained on the left wall.

As we moved into the temple we went back many centuries to Pharaonic Egypt. The walls and columns were covered in pictures of the god Khnum. One showed him being offered sacrifices by Ptolemy IV and, most lovely of all, the god being presented with a large cage of birds decorated with lotus blossoms.

The great temple of Denderah stands in isolation on the western bank of the Nile 60 kilometres north of Luxor. It is consecrated to Hathor Goddess of Love, whom the Greeks call Aphrodite and who was known under many names and symbols in ancient Egypt. Her titles included Mistress of the Gods, Lady of the Sycamore, Hathor of Thebes and Lady of the West. She represented the female power in nature, wife of the Sun God himself, and not only gave sustenance to man on earth but also during the long journey through the underworld. Sometimes she wore a sycamore emblem on her head with her hands full of flowers and fruit. At other times she was seen in the form of a cow with yet another Hathor symbol between the horns, the lunar disc backed by two large ostrich feathers.

The followers of Hathor at Denderah were famous for their peculiar abhorrence of the crocodile, at a time when it was still being worshipped in many other parts of Egypt. They had a fearless attitude towards the reptiles and were reputed to receive no harm even if swimming amongst them. The Romans wished to exhibit crocodiles in their own country and invited a number of Denderah Egyptians to act as keepers. The strange entourage went to Rome where a reservoir was built to hold the reptiles. It was edged with a platform where the Egyptians would drag the crocodiles from the water in nets so that the Romans could see them.

Denderah temple is often overlooked through its nearness to Abydos and Thebes. The walls are inscribed with the names of many Roman Emperors and it boasts one of the most famous walls ever to have been carved – portraying Cleopatra, Caesar and their son, Caesarion. It is some three miles from the town of Keneh. Outside the spacious courtyard are two gigantic wells, so deep it is difficult to tell whether they still contain water or not. A lintel incised with the wings of Horus lies over the entrance to a hall of stately proportions with a wide central aisle and three rows of pillars on each side. Instead of lotus flower capitals, each pillar, of which there are 24, is affixed to the roofing by a Hathor head. Sandwiched between each head and the ceiling are sculptured replicas of the goddess suckling a babe. Turquoise blue still adheres to the broad foreheads though much of the colouring has peeled off.

Footsteps echo across the stone flooring. Be careful to avoid the large holes where succeeding doors once hinged to and fro. The sanctuary is in the middle. In this Holy of Holies a beautiful fresco shows Hathor being proferred incense by a young Pharaoh. It is held out to the goddess on a beautifully carved artificial hand, joined to a slender staff. All temple drawings show incense being offered in this way so that the human may not come into too close proximity with a deity. One of the small chambers has its roof designed in semi-surrealistic fashion. It shows the goddess's body edging three sides. Sunrays issue from the groin and strike a sundisc, symbol of Ra, on the fourth side.

From an antechamber you can ascend a narrow staircase to a small shrine dedicated to Osiris, called the Temple on the Roof. Again the ceiling is of interest, having in the centre a face-on carving of Hathor as a woman and in a corner a blackened zodiac. The latter is a replacement by Mohamet Aly who had the original cut out and sent to Paris as a gift in 1821. It is now in the Louvre. The walls are surrounded with reliefs of a mummified Pharaoh being brought back to life by the occult powers of the God of Fertility.

When one goes downstairs to the temple one can visit a crypt beneath the floor itself, but I do not advise this for elderly people, or for those who suffer from claustrophobia. One goes down a steep ladder through a round hole and is handed a lighted candle by a guide. The passage is so narrow that one can touch both sides at once, yet the air is cool and dry, the sand fine and solid underfoot. By walking in Indian file some of the most beautiful carvings in Egypt can be seen. If there is a single flaw along the superb friezes I did not detect it. The carvings are less than quarter life size.

Horus stands alone – the perfect Horus. He is portrayed not as a man with a falcon's head, but as a hawk with beautiful plumage. As in Greek sculpture horses sometimes appear more beautiful than those of flesh and blood, so the small Horus appears more splendid than any bird of prey. The head in profile is held with dignity. The beak gleams like ivory. The god's eye is farseeing. A cascade of coloured feathers covers the plump breast, beneath which soft down can be sensed rather than seen. The graceful wing lies close to the side like a folded jewelled fan. The feathers are exquisite, each with tiny veins spreading from a tapering quill.

Picture succeeds picture. A snake, its malevolent eye shining like a diamond, its scales oily in the candlelight, slithers on the stone, too real for comfort. The fatal loveliness of Cleopatra is glimpsed in a small cameo where she nurses the infant Caesarion. The minute bodies of a Pharaoh and his Queen are seated on thrones.

Out in the courtyard the reliefs on the outer walls seem exceptionally large after the tiny cameos.

The most famous wall carving, that of Cleopatra, Caesar and their son, is seen last of all. The royal family are being blessed by four gods. Caught in the stone is the likeness of the Queen who beguiled all men including Caesar, ruler of Imperial Rome, and Mark Antony, leader of the mightiest army of the day. From this wall, the most photographed in all Egypt, Cleopatra's fatal fascination has been extolled through the years.

You cross the courtyard to see the Mammisi or House of Giving Birth, built by Augustus. A square building, it is much larger than the Temple on the Roof. On its inner walls the Goddess Hathor is shown in the various stages of giving birth.

Abydos temple is beyond the pretty little town of Baliana in the same way as Denderah is from Keneh, but in complete contrast to Denderah, Abydos is one of the oldest in Egypt. The site upon which it rests had been held in veneration for thousands of years and many temples had risen and fallen there before the present one was built. The names of the numerous gods who had been worshipped in the old shrines are many, but in the present temple homage was paid to Ahenti Amentiu or Foremost of the Westerners, a predecessor of Anubis. The worship of this god later became submerged in that of Osiris. As the cult of Osiris gained in strength, the soil under Abydos became doubly hallowed for the belief grew that when Set had hewn Osiris into pieces the head had been buried beneath it.

Pharaohs were associated with Osiris at death, for the god had become the symbol of resurrection. Later in history the nobles and priesthood were identified with the god in the same way, and by the time of the Middle Kingdom even the body of a commoner could claim affiliation with the deity.

Osiris gradually superseded all the old funerary gods.

Pilgrims came from afar to take part in religious ceremonies at Abydos, as at Philae, and it became the greatest wish of many to be laid to final rest there.

Unlike the Pharaohs who had their tombs cut into the mountainside at Thebes, other kings wished to be buried within the precincts of Abydos temple in close proximity of the godhead. These included King Djer of the first dynasty and King Sethos I of the nineteenth dynasty. The latter made doubly sure of protection in the after life by having a rock tomb and temple built at Thebes as well!

Due to its temple, Abydos became one of the most renowned places in Egypt, second only to Thebes. Magnificent tombs encroached so close to the temple that a wall had to be built to protect it. Two famous Osiris symbols were kept in the temple sanctum, one a bundle of golden flower stems and the other a large golden sceptre, the top of which was carved with a face and crowned with two ostrich feathers. Two cobras coiled above the forehead and the whole was studded with precious gems and blue faience.

The pictures which cover the walls at Abydos, commanded by Seti I are ravishingly beautiful. Delicacy in bas-relief carving reached a peak of perfection during the reign of this Pharaoh. You have the feeling that Seti knew this and therefore gave his talented artists every facility and encouragement.

The temple, built of white calcareous stone, was not completed by the time Seti died and his son Ramses II left it as it was, only adding wall decorations where there were none. These told of memorials he had erected to the memory of his father in other places.

One hall, splendidly proportioned, contains three rows of 36 columns. The walls enclosing them are resplendent with hieroglyphics and reliefs. Seven naves lead off this hall, six dedicated to individual deities. The seventh was built to the glory of Seti himself. The walls depict the Pharaoh adoring himself as a god and being carried in procession by the gods themselves. In each of the other chambers the Pharaoh is seen making sacrifices to Horus, Isis, Osiris, Amen, Marmachis and Ptah, pouring water on sacred lotus flowers, burning incense, praying and adoring.

In a roofless antechamber Seti is shown teaching his son Ramses how to lasso a wild bull. On a wall in a long gallery the famous Tablet of Abydos can be seen, that amazing catalogue of the 76 dynastic kings of ancient Egypt. Egyptologists have found this genealogical tree most helpful, and from it know that many Pharaonic tombs have not yet been uncovered. Although the tablet is not a comprehensive list and does not give the names of Pharaohs before the unification of Upper and Lower Egypt, it has proved a unique key to the past.

Motioning towards the 76 royal cartouches are two regal figures, one being Seti I. The King wears the double crown of Egypt, while clasped about his firm slender neck hangs an elongated jewelled collar. Wide bracelets are fastened around his arms at the wrists and above the elbows. A knee length pleated skirt is drawn in at the waist over which flows a fine transparent outer skirt falling to the ankles. The high arched feet are bare. One hand gestures gracefully with open tapering fingers towards the Pharaonic list, while the other holds a rod at the end of which a modelled artificial hand clutches a tiny bowl of burning incense. It is difficult to say which of the tableaux is most pleasing at Abydos, Seti offering wine to Horus, Seti just about to place a brilliantly begemmed collar around the neck of a god, or Isis holding the Key of Life to Seti's lips. Each relief seems more enchanting than the last. In one Seti holds a little bat in his hand. If the slender fingers uncurled it would surely dart away. You almost catch the fragrance of incense, the tangy smell of fruit, the scent of flowers. Very real particularly, is a carving of Seti offering an image of Truth to Osiris. The modelling of the tiny figure in the outstretched palm of the Pharaoh's hand is in itself quite exquisite. The semi curve of the small shoulder, the limbs, the upright bearing, all have sheer poetry of line. And in one tiny hand is clasped the Key of Life. In fact ugliness is non existent at Abydos. The variety of blues, apricots, reds and the delicate pastel shades with which the stone is suffused are as vivid today as when they were applied 1,400 years before the birth of Christ.

A flight of steps at the end of a long corridor leads up to an opening in the wall at the top of a sloping sandhill. At the bottom excavations are still proceeding, amongst a mass of broken walls and tombs. And the Abydos mysteries still unfold as excavations are continued year after year and two corridors of burial vaults have recently been uncovered within the temple grounds. Time is required to examine each one as every mound of sand has to be sifted carefully. The earth gives up her secrets slowly and with reluctance.

10 The Fayoum, Minia and Assiut

The reason why the Fayoum is often referred to as an oasis which is not an oasis requires explanation. It is a natural depression or valley in the desert some 60 miles south west of Cairo. In ancient times it was connected by a man-made canal to the Nile and served as a sort of accumulator absorbing water when the river was in flood and releasing it for irrigation when the river level subsided. Today the connection to the Nile is silted up and it is a true oasis relying on spring water to fill Lake Karoun and make one of the most fertile provinces of Egypt. The lake is gradually shrinking and is now well below sea level.

You can go to the Fayoum by driving from Cairo along the Pyramid Road out nearly as far as Mena House and then taking the desert road away to the right of the Pyramids. Ahead the road stretches shiny and black in a straight line. On the outskirts of the Fayoum on the left hand side you must halt to see the little museum at Kranis where there is also a rest house and a small shop. At the former you can have a meal or light refreshments and at the latter food from the Fayoum such as olives and honey can be bought.

The museum is a recent one and although small has many interesting exhibits the most fascinating perhaps being a small stone crocodile just inside the entrance. The Greeks called the Fayoum Crocodilopolis for it was sacred to the crocodile-god Sabek who was worshipped there. At Kranis museum there are several tiny ushabti figures, some in the form of mummies. Four Egyptian mummies are on display in a wonderful state of preservation and in one glass cabinet there are many tiny figures of Bast, about a quarter of an inch high. There are also examples of the famous 'Fayoum Portraits' – pictures of the heads of the deceased found in their tombs, the best of which can be seen at the Egyptian Museum in Cairo. They are Roman in date and painted in a style called eucaustic. There is nothing else like them and the best are vivid lifelike portraits of astonishing force and character. Other exhibits include gold jewellery, Roman coins and pottery.

Just beyond the museum the road cuts like a thin sword through the perpetual green of the oasis. The landscape on either side is flat like Holland and, like Holland in summer, it is lush with rich vegetable plots and water canals. Visitors to Egypt are always interested while reading menus to note that the most luscious food seems to be described as coming from 'Fayoum'. True it is that some of the finest turkeys, chickens and vegetables really do come from this vast garden in the desert. It is also a fruit-growing district and as long ago as Pharaonic times, was regarded as the 'orchard of Egypt'. There is an impressive range of almond, apricot, orange, lemon, pomegranate, fig and olive groves. Tall acacias, tamarisks and eucalyptus trees cast dappled shadows on the grass. If you stop your car and listen, you can hear the faint music of hundreds of water wheels.

The sugar cane grows high, far taller than oneself, and sometimes lurking among the tall purple stalks there is a feral cat. The white egret, too, is found everywhere in the Fayoum, following the plough or the water buffaloes or wading in the bright crystal greeness of rice paddies.

The capital of the governorate has a population of 140,000. In the centre of a traffic island in the busiest part of the town there is the obelisk of Abguig erected by King Sesostris in the twelfth dynasty. It is 13 metres tall, made of granite and is covered with pharaonic inscriptions.

Driving beyond the town once again you are conscious of lush greenery and, after many date groves and endless fields of clover, beans and other vegetables, you come to Lake Karoun on your right. It is smooth, placid and shimmering and spreads into the far distance, where its mother of pearl surface meets the pale blue sky. The marshes surrounding it are full of bird life. There is a constant chirping. Sometimes date trees and crops edge the water, at other places there is a fine white sand where fishing nets are spread to dry. There is fishing and water skiing to be had and the lake is really a sportsman's paradise.

Sometimes during the winter the water is said to be black with duck. You can watch them fly away, literally darkening the sky, in their thousands. European wild fowl tarry there on their annual migration. Not only the sportsman but the ornithologist and naturalist find the lake entrancing for it can produce every species of bird of prey, ducks (including the rare marbled duck), pelicans, cranes and storks. As the sun goes down you can sometimes notice the water in the far distance is a rosy colour, but when it moves like a great pink cloud into the sky, you know it is hundreds of flamingoes taking off into the evening light.

There are two pension type hotels at the lake's edge; the Pavillon de Chasse and the Pavillon du Lac, both with open log fireplaces and glassed-in verandahs, the latter perfect for breakfasts after an early morning shoot. Bookings are difficult at weekends. But there is nothing to stop you leaving Cairo very early and, after a two hour drive, having a day's sport and returning to the capital again, the same evening. Pigeon shooting is one thing the fellah will frown upon. He uses pigeon manure for his fields. But why bother about pigeon when there is everything else? There is shooting the year round – and many accessible places to go for it. June, July and August are the months for grouse, March, April and May for quail and wild turtledoves, September brings migratory birds along the Mediterranean. Hawking can sometimes be obtained in the desert and, in the winter season, November to the end of March, there are snipe and wild duck.

El Syllin is about ten kilometres from Fayoum and is famous for its springs of mineral water similar in taste to Vichy. The springs have now become part of a small park, a very pretty spot with a restaurant and chalets for hire nearby.

It is not as easy to have a day trip to Minia or Assiut as it is to Fayoum. Minia is 247 kilometres south of Cairo and, although you can go by train in an air-conditioned compartment in about three and a half hours or by car on a well paved road, it does not leave much time for sightseeing. Assiut is 378 kilometres distant from Cairo. Neither place has very suitable hotels for tourists at the time of going to press but both are generally part of the Nile cruise itineraries.

Minia is the capital of an extensive province and has several sugar and cotton factories as well as a large university. An engineering faculty is to be added to the four existing ones of agriculture, educational science, art and human sciences. There is a good shopping main street and an interesting souk but most attractive of all is the long winding corniche facing the Nile. I stayed at the Lotus, a pension-type hotel, where you can have meals on the roof and from there get a general idea of the layout of the town and see across the river. Among the interesting excursions are those to Beni Hassen, Tunah el Gebel and the Mallawi museum.

Across the metallic lane of the river lie the closely packed Pharaonic tombs of Beni Hassen. These burial vaults date back to the eleventh and twelfth dynasties and burrow into thick layers of fine white limestone, their walls polished and overlaid with plaster on which the scenes of the past life of the dead are painted. Most famous is Tomb No. 2 that of Ameni who was governor of the XVIth nome of Upper Egypt during the reign of Usertsen I. Ameni was hereditary prince of the district and also held the office of priest to various goddesses and gods. Architecturally his tomb is interesting in that it uses both octagonal and polyhedral pillars to support it. There are pictorial representations of the working of flint and metal, the construction of a bier and of the manufacture of bows, pottery and stone vessels. The methods of ploughing, treading corn, reaping, wine making and the weaving of rope are clearly shown. Sports such as the netting of fish and birds and wrestling together with many other facets of life in Pharaonic Egypt are also depicted.

The most colourful tomb interior at Beni Hassen is no. 17, that of Khati, overseer of the Eastern Desert and the governor of the nome of Meh. Two rows of columns are of the lotus bud variety and are painted blue, yellow and green.

Lower down the mountainside are scores of mummy pits with small chambers attached to them. Altogether there are over a thousand tombs at Beni Hassen.

I went to visit the museum at Mallawi some 12 kilometres from Minia. The route was particularly fascinating because I have never seen so many buffaloes, one of my favourite animals, in such a small area. They have been part of the fellaheen domestic life since time immemorial. They love the water and it is amusing to watch one being scrubbed in a canal because it always looks so idyllically happy. The 'gamooser' as the fellah calls the buffalo, with its elongated, narrow head, large fuzzy ears and long tufted tail, is more attractive than the cow. On the way to Mallawi it was extraordinary how such large creatures kept to their own section of ground. Each animal had a mound of green bercime to munch and about as much space as would accommodate its body when lying down. They were separated by tiny mud barriers perhaps six inches tall and I did not see one animal step out of its own little kingdom. They looked up now and then at us idly as we swept by, their black noses shining in the bright sunlight like patent leather.

The Mallawi museum is a joy to visit, not only because of its contents but also because the place is spotless. Each shining glass cabinet has a card written in English describing the exhibits as well as the usual one in Arabic. One room is full of Ibis statues of the Graeco-Roman period 300 B.C. The principal ibis is made of gilded wood with bronze legs and hindquarters. It holds its beak protectively over a little goddess. Three small wooden coffins contain ibis mummies. In another room with human mummies there were mirrors placed so that the bottoms of sarcophagi could be admired as well as the tops and sides. Two of these were unusual in that they had rectangles with large eyes and eyebrows painted on the sides as if the dead person was peering at the onlooker through the windows. Another cabinet held plaster masks with elaborate hairstyles. There were several small Isis statues some wrapped in linen, others with Horus on one knee. One figure wrapped in linen save for the breast, because Isis was suckling a baby Horus, had the goddess winking one eye. Yet another tiny cabinet contained what looked like a reddish chow dog with a charm bracelet worn as a collar. On the second floor of the museum there were many amphorae and Roman oil lamps. Samples of rugs from the Greco-Roman period seemed of much the same designs as today.

Tunah el Gebel lies some 20 miles west from Mallawi. It is a desert area in the hills near where Akhnaton built his new city of Tell el Amarna. Indeed you can see one of the boundary stelae in the cliffs to the north of this necropolis. On it is the famous mural, so often reproduced in books, showing Akhnaton and Nefertiti accompanied by their little daughters, holding up their arms in veneration to the sun; an inscription on it commemorates the founding of Tell el Amarna.

The most important building you see at Tunah el Gebel is the tomb of Petosiris, built at the beginning of the Macedonian rule about 300 B.C. First comes a vestibule the facade of which has four columns with floral capitals joined together by panels. The inside parts of the capitals retain their colours of turquoise, red and blue. The outer portions are bleached by the sun. Petosiris was high priest to Thoth and his wise sayings are inscribed on the walls and his tomb became a place of pilgrimage.

Wall carvings show Petosiris and his wife talking to their family and to priests. Their Greek tunics are quite different from Pharaonic clothing. Many of the reliefs show coppersmiths and metal workers and the weighing of gold. The actual burial chamber down a deep shaft has been closed and the coffin, the lid of which has coloured glass hieroglyphics inscriptions inlaid in wood, is now in the Egyptian Museum in Cairo.

Another interesting tomb is that belonging to Isidora who drowned in the nile in 120 B.C. She was sailing across the Nile to see her lover who waved to her from the far bank. She stood up to return his greeting and as she waved she lost her balance and fell in the river. Unable to swim she drowned. Doctor

Taha Hussein the blind minister who died recently had a rest house not far from this place. The first time he came to Isidora's tomb he asked that candles should be placed in wall niches and kept alight whenever he was staying at his rest house, as a gesture to the memory of Isidora. He thought this must be one of the earliest instances of a maiden dying for love.

There are two chambers in the tomb. High in the wall of the first behind two pillars spiralled with stone ropes like the thread of a screw, there is a sculptured shell. The marble effect is achieved by painting different colours and rubbing them down before they were dry. A Greek epigram on the wall reads: 'In truth oh Isidora, it is the Nymphs, the daughters of the waters, who built thee this chamber'.

There are many other house tombs, some two-storied like Isidora's at Tunah el Gebel and also undergound passages used for burying ibis, sacred to the god Thoth, very like the underground ibis excavations at Sakkara. Here also is what is thought to be the oldest known water wheel in Egypt.

On the way back to Mallawi we stopped at the ruins of Hermopolis, also sacred to Thoth. More mummified ibises have been found there. The ruins of this city are mostly in an attractive palm grove and consist of granite columns, some upright, others having fallen. These are all that are left of ancient temples save for mounds of rubble and gigantic blocks but they may reveal much in the next few years. Most fascinating are two gigantic statues of baboons, an animal associated with wisdom and learning like the ibis.

Southward of Tell el Amarna, where the world famous bust of Nefertiti was found which is now in the Berlin Museum, lies Assiut the official residence of the provincial governor and capital of Upper Egypt.

Assiut is about 230 miles from Cairo by train. Once again, as with so many towns along the river Nile, there is a beautiful tree-lined corniche where river passengers come ashore. The main part of the city lies in from the Nile near the foot of a mountain and is really on an island formed by a branch of the Nile. There is a shopping centre comprising both an up-to-date main street and the inevitable frontless shops. Here trade is brisk and craftsmen can be seen at work, always a fascination for the visitor.

Assiut's greatest pride is its university. Buildings are ringed with grassy lawns and flower beds. Particularly impressive was the agricultural faculty where the veterinary section had all kinds of animals housed under ideal conditions but where trees and flowers were not forgotten and the fish hatchery blended with the landscape. Most of the students are from Upper Egypt but some 9000 come from other parts. Professor Abdel Megied Osman, who has a PhD in Organic Chemistry from Liverpool University, has been lecturing at Assiut for the last 18 years. He said to me, 'If our students leave having learned not only their speciality but to have a sense of responsibility towards those they instruct in the future, that seems to me to be the important thing.'

If there is time while you are in Assiut to visit the Convent of the Virgin Mary it is easily accessible though it is half way up the mountain. The roadway climbs steeply and, once in the convent precincts you might have stepped back centuries. The main chapel is in a vast, cold cave which you reach by descending a flight of steps. After walking a little way and accustoming yourself to the darkness you enter a chapel which is a great square surrounded by mushrabia panels. Behind the altar there are ancient biblical paintings. The benches are plain with no backs, the ceiling is rough stone but the flooring beneath your feet is smooth. After a few minutes you notice that a little light filters through the mushrabia so that you can see the paintings. These are most impressive, one being of Christ taken down from the Cross and said to be over 1000 years old. Many babies are christened in this old Coptic place of worship and there are three fonts, their covers made of single wooden crosses.

11 The Suez Canal and its Townships

Aristotle, Strabo and Pliny all gave credit to the legendary Sesotris as one of the first Pharaohs to explore the possibilities of joining the Nile and the Red Sea. Certainly from the walls of Karnak temple it is known that such a canal existed during the reign of Seti I. Perhaps this waterway silted up because in 609 B.C. Pharaoh Necho decreed that another should be excavated and, according to Herodotus, 120,000 men died in the undertaking. In 521 B.C. Darius reopened the canal from Cairo to Suez.

Napoleon dreamed of going further and linking the Red Sea with the Mediterranean. He made a few attempts with his engineers while he was there but it took another Frenchman, several years later, to make the dream become a reality – Ferdinand de Lesseps.

De Lesseps had endless difficulties before achieving success but he had two major advantages. He won the Egyptian Prince Mohammed Said over to his way of thinking and the Empress Eugenie was his cousin. She was very intrigued with de Lessep's idea of linking the two seas and awakened the interest of Napoleon III. On the other hand the opinions of other important people varied. If a canal could be excavated between the two seas what would result? Floods might sweep across the land to the very heart of Egypt, for it was believed that the Red Sea and the Mediterranean were of different levels.

However de Lesseps persevered. Engineers of international repute soon dispelled the illusion that the levels of the Red Sea and the Mediterranean were significantly different. At last, with the backing of an international commission representing most of the European countries, the great scheme was begun.

During this period labour was cheap but equipment primitive and getting food for the men was difficult. Also there was the more pressing need of a water supply for drinking. The burning sun gave no relief to bronzed bodies burrowing in the sand. Thirst was the greatest problem. Camels by the hundred had to carry the water all the way from the Nile to quench parched throats and this precarious source of supply became such an outrageous expense that de Lesseps had to slow down his work to cut out a sweet water canal from Cairo to the shores of Lake Timsah, the midpoint of the canal. It was worth the extra effort and in the event saved months of precious time. Almost overnight villages sprang up along its route and, from its sweet water and rich Nile mud, the sand grew lush with vegetables and fruit trees. The new canal was then continued north and south, parallel to the navigable waterway, to provide fresh water supplies to Port Said and Suez.

Khedive Ismail had invited the Empress Eugenie to be guest of honour at the opening of the canal. She accepted eagerly as did other royal guests. Beflagged ships of all kinds and nationalities assembled in the harbour basin at Port Said, named after the Prince, to form the first convoy along the new waterway. The ships drew up in line behind Eugenie's *Aigle,* which was the first ship and cautiously they made their way through the first half of the canal to Ismailia, named after the Khedive. When the guests went ashore they were received at de Lesseps villa. That night the Khedive gave a ball to celebrate the event.

Next day the convoy reformed in line and gradually edged its way through Lake Timsah, where beduin, cheering wildly, waved them on from the banks and the ships continued on to the Great Bitter Lakes. There they dropped anchor for the night and dinner parties were given on board several ships. Next morning the ships wended their way to their final destination and by lunchtime Eugenie wrote in the logbook of the *Aigle* with a firm hand – 'Anchored at Suez'. The first convoy had passed safely through the Suez Canal. The same route was followed by convoy after convoy down through the years and during the two Great World Wars.

In the past Port Said conjured up many pictures in the imagination. It has been referred to as the Gateway to the East, where if you landed from a ship for only an hour, you had to buy leather goods, jewellery and a hundred other things. It was described as an ordinary seaport, a place of romance, a city of beach villas, green squares and exhilarating sea breezes, where watches and cameras were cheap.

As well as being a busy port Port Said was an up-to-date seaside resort and a fishing village. The artificial harbour and its quays and landing stages had a straight mole jutting out into the sea like a promenade.

Stretching along the whole Canal there were little stations like frontier posts. Enclosed by high walls, each had a small villa above which was erected a long pole of timber, like a flagstaff but draped with all the impedimenta of a ship's mast and used for signalling oncoming ships. The actual Headquarters of the Suez Canal Company was at Ismailia, midway down the canal, where the administrative staff and many of the pilots lived. Their office buildings were large and airy, the villas charming.

Much has changed along the Suez Canal since the recent bitter fighting. Ships were sunk or scuttled and it became impassable for international shipping. Fifteen vessels flying the flags of eight different countries were trapped in the lakes and the canal became the front line. For eight years the famous waterway ceased to function. Then as suddenly as the fighting began it ceased. On the 5th June 1975 the canal was formally reopened by President Sadat to international shipping, its waters having been cleared by the combined efforts of the Egyptians and units from several of the great navies of the world. Wrecks have been removed, mines blown up and dredging has halted the encroaching sand. The ships nose their way past the three townships which are coming back to life.

Hundreds of new flats have been built at Suez and Port Said

and the harbours have been enlarged, the docks and workships are being rebuilt and bomb damage has been cleared away. The World Bank has subscribed 280 million dollars for reconstruction.

I visited Ismailia recently and went to de Lesseps villa. It still stands in its spacious garden. I went through the quiet rooms, fingered the mosquito net of his four-poster bed, smiled as I saw his grey marble topped washstand with its silver basin and brass ewer which might have been used yesterday. Behind his simple desk faded pictures hung on the wall showing family portraits and the opening of the canal in 1869. I wondered when I saw the small vessels what de Lesseps would have thought of the larger ones like the 30,000 tons container ships that go through the waterway today. Indeed there are ambitious plans to widen and deepen the canal to take the latest super tankers within the next few years. A free port and duty free area are also under consideration and the recreational potential of the canal is being explored.

APPENDIX A

As there are only ten numbers to remember in Arabic it is worthwhile to learn them. Bus numbers are in Arabic, price tags in shops also (these are government controlled) so it is useful to be able to decipher them.

ARABIC NUMBERS

1	WAHID	١
2	ECKNEEN	٢
3	TALATA	٣
4	ARBAA	٤
5	KHAMSA	٥
6	SITTA	٦
7	SABBA	٧
8	TAMANYA	٨
9	TESSA	٩
10	ASHRA	١٠

APPENDIX B

Useful words in Arabic spelt phonetically

Yes	Aheewa
No	La
How much	Becalm
Good day	Sa-eeda
Never mind	Marleesh
Please	Men Fadlak
Thank you	Macheckra or shookrarn
Stop	Stanner Shwyer
Little	Shwyer
Possible	Moomkin
Not possible	Moosh Moomkin
That's all	Bus
Right	Yemeen
Left	Shemari
Money	Feloose
Give Me	Eddeenie
Bring me	Hatli
Here	Henna
Listen	Ismah
I do not have	Mafeesh
Taxi	Taxi
Bus	Autobus
Good	Quise
Milk	Layban
Sugar	Sooker
Tea	Shy
Coffee	Ahwa
Water	Moya
Street	Sharia
Village	Ezba

Index

190